CREATIVE CHEESE

Provides an exciting variety of ⸴
occasions, and shows how you can ⸴⸴⸴ ⸴⸴⸴⸴ your own
cheeses at home using fresh, natural ingredients.

Creative
CHEESE
COOKERY

How to Cook with and Make Rennet-free Cheeses

Jo Marcangelo

Illustrated by Kim Blundell

THORSONS PUBLISHERS LIMITED
Wellingborough, Northamptonshire.

First published 1985

© JO MARCANGELO 1985

British Library Cataloguing in Publication Data

Marcangelo, Jo
   Creative cheese cookery.
   1. Cookery (Cheese)
   I. Title
   641.6'73   TX759

   ISBN 0-7225-0945-6

Printed and bound in Great Britain by
Anchor Brendon Ltd, Tiptree, Essex

Contents

	Page
Acknowledgements	7
Introduction	9

PART ONE: COOKING WITH SOFT CHEESE

Chapter

1. Starters and Snacks	13
2. Main-course Dishes	40
3. Salads and Salad Dressings	64
4. Puddings and Desserts	78
5. Cheesecakes	98

PART TWO: HOME-MADE CHEESES

6. An Introduction to Cheesemaking	117
7. Ingredients	120
8. Cheesemaking Equipment	122
9. Cheesemaking Recipes	127
Glossary	153
Useful Addresses	157
Index	159

Acknowledgements

I would like to thank the staff at Neal's Yard Dairy, Covent Garden, London WC2 for their help and advice on making soft cheeses. Many thanks to Messrs. Fullwood and Bland Limited and also Lotus Foods Limited, suppliers of vegetarian rennet.

Introduction

Versatile, tasty and nutritious, cheese is a cook's best friend. It is the natural way to preserve the food value of milk. Cheese is an important source of protein for lacto-vegetarians and it offers almost endless variety in cooking. It is also rich in calcium, riboflavin and vitamin A. But, with the exception of such low-fat cheeses as cottage cheese, it is also high in saturated fat and cholesterol. For this reason, most of the recipes in this book have been developed using low-fat soft cheeses and wholefood ingredients. Soft cheeses, in particular, are so mild-tasting that they combine well with many other ingredients, both savoury and sweet, to produce a variety of interesting, wholesome dishes.

For readers who would like to try making their own cheeses at home, the second part of this book clearly explains the steps and principles involved. The instructions for making cheese may sound complicated, but the process is not as difficult as it seems. For your first attempts, choose cheeses that are made with small quantities of milk. These give a greater yield per measure of milk, are relatively simple to make and do not require expensive equipment. By making cheese at home, you will not only be able to learn a satisfying craft, but will also be rewarded with the fact that your products are unprocessed and free from harmful additives and preservatives.

As you gain confidence you will learn the variables of cheesemaking, such as using full-fat milk or skimmed milk; heating the milk to a higher or lower temperature; adding more or less rennet, scalding the curd etc. All these variables affect the finished product and produce the many varieties of flavour and texture. The more you learn about it, the more fascinating cheesemaking becomes.

Soft Cheese
In Britain soft cheeses are divided into six grades, depending on their butterfat content (how much fat they contain), and the Trade Descriptions Act has laid down what each grade of cheese must be called. The grades are:

less than 2% butterfat.......skimmed milk soft cheese
2-10% butterfat...............low-fat soft cheese
10-20% butterfat.............medium-fat soft cheese
20-45% butterfat.............full-fat soft cheese
45-65% butterfat.............cream cheese*
over 65% butterfat...........double cream cheese*

The names low-fat, medium-fat and so on are now printed on the packets or cartons of most soft cheeses, foreign as well as British, so you can swap one brand for another of the same grade. Go by the grade names (low-fat etc.) not the butterfat percentages which are calculated in different ways in different countries.

When using soft cheese for cooking it is important to buy exactly the type stated in the recipe. Suitability greatly depends on the texture and composition of a cheese, particularly its proportion of fat and water. You can use home-made or bought cheese for the recipes in this book, provided they are the right grade for the recipe. Whether you buy or make the soft cheese, it will only keep in the refrigerator for a few days. Although soft cheeses were invented as a way of preserving milk, they are a very short-term preserve. Always check the sell-by date or ask the shop. Most full-fat and medium-fat curd and cream cheeses can be frozen but low-fat and skimmed milk varieties do not freeze well.

*Cream cheeses are seldom true cheeses; usually they are not made from curds, but from drained, set cream.

PART ONE: COOKING WITH SOFT CHEESE

1.
STARTERS AND SNACKS

SCRAMBLED (BUTTERED) EGGS WITH COTTAGE CHEESE

(Serves 3-4)

Imperial (metric)	American
4 eggs	4 eggs
Sea salt and freshly ground black pepper	Sea salt and freshly ground black pepper
½oz (15g) butter or vegetable margarine	1 tablespoon butter or vegetable margarine
4oz (100g) cottage cheese	½ cup cottage cheese
3-4 thick slices wholemeal bread	3-4 thick slices wholewheat bread
Sprigs of watercress	Sprigs of watercress

1. Beat the eggs lightly and season with salt and pepper to taste.

2. Melt the butter or margarine in a pan over a low heat and tip in the eggs. Scramble (cook) very slowly, scraping the bottom of the pan with a wooden spatula, until they form a soft clot. Stir in the cottage cheese and continue to cook over low heat until the cheese is heated through.

3. Meanwhile, toast the bread. Divide the scrambled eggs among the pieces of toast. Garnish with sprigs of watercress and serve immediately.

Variation: Add chopped fresh herbs to the eggs, or add a pinch of paprika or curry powder.

COTTAGE CHEESE OMELETTE

(Serves 4)

Imperial (metric)	American
4 oz (100g) cottage cheese	½ cup cottage cheese
4 eggs, separated	4 eggs, separated
1-2 tablespoons chopped parsley or chervil	1-2 tablespoons chopped parsley or chervil
Sea salt and freshly ground black pepper	Sea salt and freshly ground black pepper
1 oz (25g) butter or polyunsaturated margarine	2 tablespoons butter or polyunsaturated margarine

1. Light the grill (broiler) or preheat the oven to 425°F/ 220°C (Gas Mark 7).

2. Sieve the cottage cheese into a bowl, lightly beat in the egg yolks, parsley or chervil and seasoning to taste. Whisk the egg whites until stiff enough to stand up in peaks but not dry, then fold them into the mixture.

3. Melt the butter in a 10 inch (25 cm) omelette pan or heavy frying pan (skillet) until it begins to foam. Before it turns colour pour in the omelette mixture. Cook over a low heat until brown underneath and beginning to puff up in the pan. Finish cooking the omelette in the oven until brown on top, or set it under the grill (broiler) for 1-2 minutes. Fold the omelette in half and slide it onto a warm plate. Serve immediately.

COTTAGE CHEESE BREAD

(Makes 2 loaves)

Imperial (Metric)	American
1 lb (450g) wholemeal flour	4 cups wholewheat flour
1 teaspoon sea salt	1 teaspoon sea salt
8 oz (225g) cottage cheese	1 cup cottage cheese
½ oz (15g) fresh yeast	1 tablespoon fresh yeast
7 fl oz (200 ml) warm water	¾ cup warm water
Beaten egg or milk to glaze	Beaten egg or milk to glaze
Sesame seeds, for sprinkling	Sesame seeds, for sprinkling

1. Mix the flour and salt together in a mixing bowl. Sieve the cottage cheese, then mix with the flour.

2. Cream the yeast with a little of the water and leave until frothy. Add to the flour mixture with just enough of the remaining water, and mix thoroughly to make a fairly firm dough.

3. Turn onto a floured surface and knead well – about 10 minutes. Place in a clean bowl, cover with a damp cloth and leave to rise in a warm place for about 2 hours, until doubled in size.

4. Knock back the dough, knead it for a few minutes, then divide it in half. Shape each half into a long roll and place on a greased baking sheet. Use a sharp knife to make slits slantwise along the length of the loaves. Cover and leave to rise in a warm place for about 30 minutes until almost doubled in size.

5. Brush with beaten egg or milk and sprinkle sesame seeds on the top. Bake the loaves in the centre of a preheated hot oven, 425°F/220°C (Gas Mark 7) for 25-30 minutes, until golden brown and the loaves sound hollow when tapped underneath. Turn onto a wire rack to cool. Eat very fresh.

BUTTERMILK SCONES WITH CREAM CHEESE AND CHIVES

(Makes 10 scones)

Imperial (Metric)	American
8oz (225g) wholemeal flour	2 cups wholewheat flour
Pinch of sea salt	Pinch of sea salt
1 teaspoon baking powder	1 teaspoon baking soda
2oz (50g) butter or vegetable margarine	¼ cup butter or vegetable margarine
¼ pint (150 ml) cultured buttermilk	⅔ cup cultured buttermilk
A little beaten egg or milk for brushing scones	A little beaten egg or milk for brushing scones
4-6oz (100-175g) single cream cheese (see page 132)	½-¾ cup light cream cheese (see page 132)
2 tablespoons finely chopped chives	2 tablespoons finely chopped chives
¼ clove of garlic, peeled and crushed (optional)	¼ clove of garlic, peeled and crushed (optional)

1. Sieve the flour, salt and baking powder into a large mixing bowl, and add the bran from the sieve. Rub in the fat until the mixture resembles breadcrumbs. Add the buttermilk and mix thoroughly to form a soft dough.

2. Turn out onto a floured surface and knead very lightly until smooth. Roll out the dough thickly (about 1 inch/2 cm thick). Cut into rounds and place on a lightly oiled baking tray.

3. Brush the scones with beaten egg or milk and bake in a preheated hot oven, 425°F/220°C (Gas Mark 7) for 12-15 minutes. Turn onto a wire rack to cool slightly.

4. Mix together the cream cheese, chives and garlic, if using. Break the scones apart while still warm, split each one and spread with the cheese mixture. Serve immediately.

Variation: Use natural yogurt in place of the cultured buttermilk.

TOMATO AND COTTAGE CHEESE COCKTAIL

(Serves 2-3)

Imperial (Metric)
½ pint (300 ml) tomato juice,
   tinned or freshly made
2 oz (50g) cottage cheese
1 stick of celery
½ green pepper, deseeded
   (optional)
½ small onion (optional)
Sea salt and freshly ground
   black pepper
Whey or water to dilute
Celery leaves to garnish

American
1⅓ cups tomato juice, tinned
   or freshly made
¼ cup cottage cheese
1 stalk of celery
½ green pepper, deseeded
   (optional)
½ small onion (optional)
Sea salt and freshly ground
   black pepper
Whey or water to dilute
Celery leaves to garnish

1. Put all the ingredients into a blender and mix together
   for approximately 1 minute.

2. Dilute with whey or water if necessary, taste and adjust
   the seasoning, place in the refrigerator to chill.

3. Pour into 2 or 3 glasses and garnish with celery leaves.

CUCUMBER AND YOGURT CHEESE DIP

(Serves 4)

Imperial (Metric)	American
1 small cucumber	1 small cucumber
8oz (225g) fresh yogurt cheese	1 cup fresh yogurt cheese
1 teaspoon onion, finely chopped	1 teaspoon onion, finely chopped
1 clove of garlic, peeled and crushed	1 clove of garlic, peeled and crushed
1-2 teaspoons chopped mint	1-2 teaspoons chopped mint
Sea salt and freshly ground black pepper	Sea salt and freshly ground black pepper

1. Wipe the cucumber clean, trim off the ends and dice finely – there is no need to remove the skin.

2. Place the fresh curds in a bowl and beat until smooth. Stir in the diced cucumber, chopped onion, crushed garlic and mint. Season to taste and turn into a small dish. Chill for an hour or two before serving.

STUFFED PEARS

(Serves 4)

Imperial (Metric)	American
4 ripe dessert pears	4 ripe dessert pears
Lemon juice	Lemon juice
8oz (225g) cottage or low-fat curd cheese	1 cup cottage or low-fat curd cheese
¼ small pineapple	¼ small pineapple
A few crisp lettuce leaves	A few crisp lettuce leaves

1. Peel the pears, cut in half and remove the cores, using a teaspoon. Brush with lemon juice to prevent them from turning brown.

2. Place the cottage cheese in a bowl. Chop the pineapple finely and add to the cheese.

3. Fill the pear cavities with the cottage cheese and pineapple mixture and place on top of the lettuce on four individual serving plates. Chill before serving.

CHEESE-STUFFED PRUNES

(Makes about 24)

Imperial (Metric)	American
8 oz (225g) dried prunes (about 24 prunes)	8 ounces dried prunes (about 24 prunes)
8 oz (225g) low-fat curd cheese	1 cup low-fat curd cheese
2 tablespoons honey	2 tablespoons honey
About 24 blanched almonds, toasted	About 24 blanched almonds, toasted

1. Place the prunes in a bowl. Cover with plenty of cold water and leave to soak for 6 hours or until they are plump but not mushy. Drain on kitchen paper. Make a slit down one side of each prune and remove the stones, taking care not to open them too much.

2. In a separate bowl, mix together the cheese and honey, then spoon in a heaped teaspoon of the mixture into each prune, allowing a generous amount to project over the top. Decorate each prune with a toasted almond. Serve chilled.

Variation: Use apricots instead of prunes.

CREAM CHEESE-STUFFED DATES

(Makes about 30)

Imperial (Metric)	American
1 lb (450g) fresh dates	1 pound fresh dates
8 oz (225g) cream cheese (approx.)	1 cup cream cheese (approx.)
Paprika and fresh chopped parsley to sprinkle	Paprika and fresh chopped parsley to sprinkle

1. Cut slits down lengths of dates and remove stones.

2. Beat the cream cheese with a wooden spoon to soften. Place in a piping bag fitted with a medium star nozzle and pipe into the centre of the dates.

3. Sprinkle with paprika or chopped parsley. Place the dates in small sweet cases and serve.

STUFFED CUCUMBER RINGS

(Serves 8)

Imperial (Metric)	American
1 large cucumber, about 16 inches (40cm)	1 large cucumber, about 16 inches long
Sea salt	Sea salt
1 red eating apple	1 red eating apple
4oz (100g) low-fat curd cheese	½ cup low-fat curd cheese
½ green pepper, deseeded and chopped	½ green pepper, deseeded and chopped
1-2 tablespoons mayonnaise	1-2 tablespoons mayonnaise
Freshly ground black pepper	Freshly ground black pepper
Sprigs of parsley to garnish	Sprigs of parsley to garnish

1. Remove both ends from the cucumber, cut eight thin slices and reserve for garnish.

2. Cut the cucumber into eight equal pieces, then scoop out all the seeds with a serrated teaspoon or a grapefruit knife. Sprinkle the insides with salt and leave upside down on kitchen paper to drain for half an hour.

3. Core and chop the apple, but do not peel. Place in a bowl with the curd cheese, green pepper and mayonnaise and mix well. Season to taste. Spoon into the cucumber cups and garnish with the reserved cucumber slices and sprigs of parsley. Serve on a bed of lettuce, or as a cocktail snack.

STUFFED EGGS

(Serves 6)

Imperial (Metric)	American
6 eggs (hard-boiled and shelled)	6 eggs (hard-cooked and shelled)
4oz (100g) acid-curd cheese	½ cup acid-curd cheese
3-4 tablespoons natural yogurt	3-4 tablespoons plain yogurt
½ teaspoon lemon juice	½ teaspoon lemon juice
Sea salt and freshly ground black pepper	Sea salt and freshly ground black pepper
2 tablespoons chopped chives	2 tablespoons chopped chives
1 tablespoon chopped dill	1 tablespoon chopped dill
1 tablespoon chopped tarragon	1 tablespoon chopped tarragon
½ Cos lettuce, shredded	½ Romaine lettuce, shredded

1. Cut the eggs in half lengthwise and scoop out the yolks, being careful not to damage the whites.

2. Mash the cheese and egg yolks together with a fork, add the yogurt, lemon juice and salt and pepper to taste; mix well. Stir in the chopped herbs. Spoon or pipe the mixture into the egg white halves.

3. Arrange the lettuce on a serving plate and place the eggs on top.

CREAMY TOMATO SOUP

(Serves 4-6)

Imperial (Metric)	American
2 carrots	2 carrots
2 large onions	2 large onions
1oz (25g) butter or polyunsaturated margarine	2 tablespoons butter or polyunsaturated margarine
2 tablespoons wholemeal flour	2 tablespoons wholewheat flour
1½lbs (675g) tomatoes, peeled and quartered	1½ pounds tomatoes, peeled and quartered
1 bay leaf	1 bay leaf
2 tablespoons tomato purée	2 tablespoons tomato paste
1½ pints (900 ml) water or stock	3¾ cups water or stock
A little raw cane sugar (optional)	A little raw cane sugar (optional)
Sea salt and freshly ground black pepper	Sea salt and freshly ground black pepper
4oz (100g) full-fat soft or cream cheese	½ cup full-fat soft or cream cheese

1. Scrape and chop the carrots. Peel and chop the onions. Melt the butter or margarine in a large saucepan, add carrots and onions and fry until the onion is transparent – about 5 minutes, but do not allow to brown.

2. Add the flour and cook, stirring for 1 minute. Add the tomatoes, bay leaf, tomato purée (paste), water or stock, sugar (if used), pepper and salt. Cover and simmer for 1 hour until vegetables are soft.

3. Remove the bay leaf, allow to cool slightly before blending in a liquidizer or food processor. Alternatively push through a sieve or food mill.

4. Return to the pan and adjust seasoning to taste. Stir in the cream cheese and reheat to serving temperature without boiling.

CHEESE BALLS

Imperial (Metric)	American
4oz (100g) Gorgonzola or other blue cheese, crumbled	1 cup Gorgonzola or other blue cheese, crumbled
8oz (225g) full-fat soft or cream cheese	1 cup full-fat soft or cream cheese
2oz (50g) chopped walnuts	½ cup chopped English walnuts

1. Mash Gorgonzola and beat into the cream cheese, then chill for 2 hours, until firm.

2. Form the cheese into small balls, and roll each one in the chopped nuts. Chill slightly, then serve on cocktail sticks.

Variation: CHEESE BONBONS – form the cheese into small balls, then place between halves of walnuts. Chill before serving.

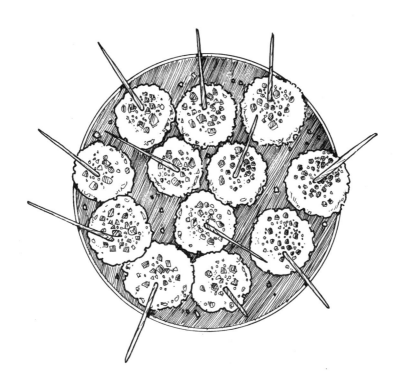

AVOCADO AND COTTAGE CHEESE PÂTÉ

(Serves 4)

Imperial (Metric)	American
2 ripe avocado pears	2 ripe avocado pears
Juice of ½ lemon	Juice of ½ lemon
2 hard-boiled eggs, shelled	2 hard-cooked eggs, shelled
4oz (100g) cottage or low-fat curd cheese	½ cup cottage or low-fat curd cheese
1 clove of garlic, peeled and crushed (optional)	1 clove of garlic, peeled and crushed (optional)
2 tablespoons mayonnaise	2 tablespoons mayonnaise
1 teaspoon finely chopped chives	1 teaspoon finely chopped chives
Sea salt and freshly ground black pepper	Sea salt and freshly ground black pepper

To garnish:	*To garnish*:
8 lettuce leaves	8 lettuce leaves
4 twists of lemon	4 twists of lemon
4 sprigs of parsley	4 sprigs of parsley

1. Cut round the avocados lengthwise, twist each into two halves and discard the stones. With a teaspoon carefully scoop out the flesh into a mixing bowl and finely mash it with the lemon juice. Reserve the shells.

2. Sieve the hard-boiled eggs and cottage cheese, then mix with the avocado and garlic (if using). Stir in the mayonnaise and chives, and season with salt and pepper to taste. (If preferred, all the ingredients may be blended until smooth in a blender or food processor.) Spoon the mixture back into the skins and roughen the surface with a fork.

3. Arrange the lettuce leaves on four individual serving dishes. Place a stuffed avocado half on top and garnish each portion with a twist of lemon and a sprig of parsley. Serve at once.

Note: When preparing avocado pears use stainless steel, ceramic or wooden utensils because some metals tend to turn the avocados an unhealthy-looking black.

AVOCADO AND YOGURT CHEESE DIP

(Serves 4-6)

Imperial (Metric)	American
2 ripe avocado pears	2 ripe avocado pears
Juice of ½ lemon	Juice of ½ lemon
8oz (225g) yogurt cheese	1 cup yogurt cheese
1 teaspoon finely chopped onion	1 teaspoon finely chopped onion
1 clove of garlic, peeled and crushed	1 clove of garlic, peeled and crushed
Sea salt and freshly ground black pepper	Sea salt and freshly ground black pepper

1. Halve the avocados and remove the stones. Scoop the flesh into a bowl and mash with the lemon juice.

2. Add the yogurt cheese, onion, garlic and salt and pepper to taste. Beat thoroughly until smooth and turn into a serving dish. (For the best results mix the ingredients in a blender or food processor.)

3. Place the dish on a large plate surrounded with fingers of crisp vegetables – carrot, celery, etc., for dipping.

STUFFED TOMATOES

(Serves 6)

Imperial (Metric)	American
6 large, firm tomatoes	6 large, firm tomatoes
4oz (100g) acid-curd or low-fat soft cheese	½ cup acid-curd or low-fat soft cheese
2 sticks of celery, chopped	2 celery stalks, chopped
1 green eating apple	1 green eating apple
1 teaspoon lemon juice	1 teaspoon lemon juice
1 spring onion or 1 tablespoon chives chopped	1 scallion or 1 tablespoon chives chopped
2 tablespoons natural yogurt	2 tablespoons plain yogurt
Sea salt and freshly ground black pepper	Sea salt and freshly ground black pepper
Sprigs of parsley to garnish	Sprigs of parsley to garnish

1. Wash and dry the tomatoes. Cut a 'lid' off the top of each and scoop out the pulp, discarding the seeds and fibrous cores. Leave the tomato shells upside down on kitchen paper to drain.

2. Mix the tomato pulp with the curd cheese, celery, chopped apple, lemon juice and spring onion or chives. Stir in the yogurt and season to taste.

3. Fill the tomatoes with the cheese mixture, replace the lids and refrigerate until required. Garnish each one with a sprig of parsley just before serving.

HOT STUFFED AVOCADO

(Serves 4)

Imperial (Metric)	American
2 large ripe avocados	2 large ripe avocados
4oz (100g) curd cheese	½ cup curd cheese
½ green pepper, chopped	½ green pepper, chopped
2 medium-sized tomatoes, skinned, seeded and chopped	2 medium-sized tomatoes, skinned, seeded and chopped
Sea salt	Sea salt
Paprika pepper	Paprika pepper
1 lemon, cut into wedges	1 lemon, cut into wedges

1. With a sharp knife, cut the avocados in half and remove the stones. Carefully scoop out the avocado flesh, leaving the skins intact, and transfer the flesh to a mixing bowl. Reserve the shells.

2. Using a fork, mash the avocado flesh with the curd cheese until smooth, then mix in the green pepper, tomatoes and salt to taste. Spoon back into the skins and sprinkle with paprika on top. Arrange in a shallow ovenproof dish.

3. Bake in a preheated moderately hot oven, 375°F/190°C (Gas Mark 5) for 15 minutes, or until the avocado is heated through. Serve with wedges of lemon.

CURRIED COTTAGE CHEESE DIP WITH CRUDITÉS

(Serves 4-6)

Imperial (Metric)	American
8oz (225g) cottage or low-fat curd cheese	1 cup cottage or low-fat curd cheese
¼ pint (150ml) soured cream or natural yogurt	⅔ cups sour cream or plain yogurt
½ teaspoon curry powder	½ teaspoon curry powder
1 clove of garlic, peeled and crushed (optional)	1 clove of garlic, peeled and crushed (optional)
Sea salt and freshly ground black pepper	Sea salt and freshly ground black pepper

For the crudités:	*For the crudités:*
½ small cauliflower	½ small cauliflower
4 carrots	4 carrots
3 sticks of celery	3 celery stalks
½ cucumber	½ cucumber
1 small head fennel	1 small head fennel
1 green and 1 red pepper, cored and seeded	1 green and 1 red pepper, cored and seeded

1. Combine all of the dip ingredients in a bowl, adding salt and pepper to taste; mix well.

2. Break the cauliflower into florets and cut the remaining vegetables into matchstick pieces.

3. Serve the dip in a small dish in the centre of a large plate, arrange the crudités round the edge.

CURD CHEESE AND OLIVE SPREAD

Imperial (Metric)	American
8oz (225g) medium-fat curd cheese	1 cup medium-fat curd cheese
2 tablespoons natural yogurt	2 tablespoons plain yogurt
12 black olives, stoned and coarsely chopped	12 black olives, pitted and coarsely chopped

1. Mash the curd cheese with the yogurt, then add the chopped olives and distribute them evenly. Use for a sandwich spread or for open sandwiches.

COTTAGE CHEESE WITH CHIVES AND SPRING ONIONS

Imperial (Metric)	American
8oz (225g) cottage cheese	1 cup cottage cheese
2 tablespoons finely chopped chives	2 tablespoons finely chopped chives
2 tablespoons chopped spring onions	2 tablespoons chopped scallions

1. Mix all the ingredients together and use as a sandwich filling.

SAVOURY CHOUX BUNS

(Makes approximately 25-30 buns)

Imperial (Metric)	American
For the choux pastry:	*For the choux pastry:*
5 oz (150g) 85% wholemeal flour	1¼ cups 85% wholewheat flour
4 oz (100g) butter or polyunsaturated margarine	½ cup butter or polyunsaturated margarine
½ pint (300 ml) cold water	1⅓ cups water
3 eggs, well beaten	3 eggs, well beaten
For the filling:	*For the filling:*
4 oz (100g) low-fat curd cheese	½ cup low-fat curd cheese
4 oz (100g) matured Cheddar cheese, finely grated	1 cup matured Cheddar cheese, finely grated
Pinch of cayenne pepper	Pinch of cayenne pepper
Pinch of dry mustard	Pinch of dry mustard
1 tablespoon chopped parsley	1 tablespoon chopped parsley
Sea salt and freshly ground black pepper	Sea salt and freshly ground black pepper
6 tablespoons double cream, whipped	6 tablespoons heavy cream, whipped
To garnish:	*To garnish:*
Yeast extract	Yeast extract
Paprika pepper	Paprika pepper
Fresh parsley, finely chopped	Fresh parsley, finely chopped

1. Sieve the flour setting aside any bran left in the sieve. Weigh sifted flour carefully then place on a piece of paper.

2. Melt the fat in the water in a medium saucepan over gentle heat. Do not allow the water to boil before the fat has melted as it will evaporate and reduce the quantity. Then bring the mixture to a rapid boil, remove the pan from the heat and tip in the flour all at once. Beat vigorously with a wooden spoon until the mixture leaves the sides of the pan clean and forms a ball.

3. Allow to cool slightly, then add the eggs a little at a time, beating well after each addition. The choux paste should be glossy and firm enough to hold its shape and you may not need to use all the eggs.

4. Pipe or spoon the mixture onto a greased baking sheet to form small buns. Leave sufficient space between the buns to allow for expansion. Bake in a preheated oven at 400°F/200°C (Gas Mark 6) for 15-20 minutes, until risen and golden brown. They should be hollow and fairly dry. Make a slit in the side of each bun to allow the steam to escape. Transfer to a wire rack to cool.

5. Meanwhile, make the filling. Place the curd cheese in a bowl and blend in the Cheddar, cayenne, mustard, parsley, and salt and pepper to taste. Fold in the cream.

6. Fill the buns with the cheese mixture. Spread each bun with a little yeast extract and dip into chopped parsley or sprinkle with paprika pepper.

LIPTAUER CHEESE

(Serves 6-8)

Imperial (Metric)	American
8oz (225g) butter, softened	1 cup butter, softened
8oz (225g) sieved cottage or low-fat curd cheese	1 cup sieved cottage or low-fat curd cheese
½ teaspoon caraway seeds, crushed	½ teaspoon caraway seeds, crushed
1 teaspoon French mustard	1 teaspoon French mustard
1 tablespoon finely chopped chives	1 tablespoon finely chopped chives
1 tablespoon chopped capers	1 tablespoon chopped capers
1½ teaspoons mild paprika pepper	1½ teaspoons mild paprika pepper

1. Cream the butter until light, then gradually work in the cheese. Add all the remaining ingredients and beat lightly until well blended.

2. Turn into a serving dish and dust lightly with paprika. Serve with rye bread, pumpernickle or toasted wholemeal bread.

COTTAGE CHEESE, DATE AND WALNUT SPREAD

Imperial (Metric)	American
8 oz (225g) cottage cheese	1 cup cottage cheese
2 oz (50g) chopped dates, with stones removed	⅓ cup chopped dates, with stones removed
2 oz (50g) chopped walnuts	½ cup chopped English walnuts
Pinch of ground cinnamon	Pinch of ground cinnamon

1. Sieve or mash the cottage cheese, then mix with the walnuts, dates and add cinnamon to taste.

YOGURT CHEESE OLIVES

(Makes about 16)

Imperial (Metric)	American
8 oz (225g) yogurt cheese	1 cup yogurt cheese
16 Spanish stuffed green olives	16 Spanish stuffed green olives
2 oz (50g) chopped hazelnuts	½ cup chopped hazelnuts
Cocktail sticks	Cocktail sticks

1. Divide the cheese into ½ oz (15g) balls and mould each round an olive.

2. Roll in the chopped nuts. Chill slightly, then serve on cocktail sticks.

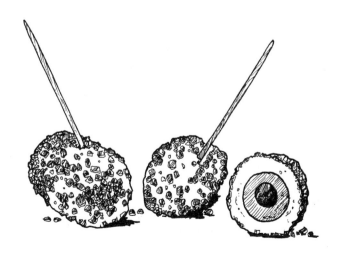

JACKET POTATOES WITH COTTAGE CHEESE AND PINEAPPLE

(Serves 4)

Imperial (Metric)	American
4oz (100g) cottage cheese	½ cup cottage cheese
2 tablespoons 'top of the milk'	2 tablespoons 'half-and-half'
¼ small pineapple, finely chopped	¼ small pineapple, finely chopped
Sea salt and freshly ground black pepper	Sea salt and freshly ground black pepper
4 large cooked jacket potatoes (see page 38)	4 large cooked jacket potatoes (see page 38)
1 tablespoon finely chopped chives	1 tablespoon finely chopped chives

1. Place the cheese in a bowl and mash with a fork. Blend in the 'top of the milk' ('half and half'), then fold in the chopped pineapple and add salt and pepper to taste.

2. Cut a large cross in the centre of each cooked potato and squeeze out some of the potato.

3. Put a large dollop of the filling in each and sprinkle with the chopped chives to serve.

AUBERGINE (EGGPLANT) SPREAD/DIP

(Serves 4)

Imperial (Metric)	American
1 large aubergine (about 8oz/225g)	1 large eggplant (about 8 ounces
8oz (225g) medium-fat curd cheese	1 cup medium-fat curd cheese
4-5 spring onions (white part only finely chopped)	4-5 scallions (white part only finely chopped)
1 tomato, peeled and chopped	1 tomato, peeled and chopped
1 tablespoon chopped parsley	1 tablespoon chopped parsley
Sea salt and freshly ground black pepper	Sea salt and freshly ground black pepper

1. Prick the aubergine (eggplant) all over with a fork, then bake in a preheated moderately hot oven 375°F/ 190°C (Gas Mark 5) for 40-50 minutes, or until it collapses and is really tender. Take out of the oven and set aside to cool.

2. Cut the aubergine (eggplant) in half lengthways and scoop out the flesh with a teaspoon. Mash the flesh with a fork in a bowl and mix in the curd cheese. Stir in the spring onions (scallions), tomato, parsley and salt and pepper to taste. To serve as a spread, use on black rye or wholemeal bread and decorate with black olives.

3. To serve as a dip, pile into a serving dish on a plate and surround the dip with a selection of savoury biscuits and raw vegetables such as red and green peppers, carrots, celery, cucumber, cauliflower florets and radishes.

Note: Part of the curd cheese can be substituted by yogurt cheese, if desired.

CREAM CHEESE AND YOGURT DIP

Imperial (Metric)	American
¼ pint (150 ml) natural yogurt	⅔ cup plain yogurt
4 oz (100g) cream cheese	½ cup cream cheese
2 tablespoons finely chopped cucumber	2 tablespoons finely chopped cucumber
1 level teaspoon paprika	1 level teaspoon paprika
Sea salt and freshly ground black pepper	Sea salt and freshly ground black pepper

1. Mix the yogurt and the cream cheese together thoroughly.

2. Stir in the cucumber and paprika. Mix well. Season to taste. Spoon into a serving dish and chill.

3. Serve with a selection of savoury biscuits and raw vegetables, such as red and green peppers, carrots, celery, chicory (endive) and fennel.

MUSHROOM DIP

Imperial (Metric)	American
12 oz (350g) yogurt cheese or other soft cheese of choice	1½ cups yogurt cheese or other soft cheese of choice
6-7 spring onions, finely chopped	6-7 scallions, finely chopped
1¼ teaspoons paprika	1¼ teaspoons paprika
Sea salt and freshly ground black pepper	Sea salt and freshly ground black pepper
4 oz (100g) button mushrooms	2 cups button mushrooms

1. Place the cheese in a mixing bowl. Stir in the spring onions (scallions), and all but ¼ teaspoon of the paprika, and seasoning to taste.

2. Wipe the mushrooms. Slice thinly and add to the dip.

3. Put into a serving dish, sprinkle the remaining paprika over and serve with crisp raw vegetables for dipping.

ONION AND CUCUMBER DIP

Imperial (Metric)	American
4oz (100g) cottage cheese, sieved	½ cup cottage cheese, sieved
3 spring onions, finely chopped	3 scallions, finely chopped
2 inches (5 cm) cucumber, finely chopped	2 inches cucumber, finely chopped
Pinch of cayenne pepper	Pinch of cayenne pepper

1. Blend all the ingredients together. Place in a serving bowl.

2. Serve with a selection of savoury biscuits and raw vegetables, such as red and green peppers, carrots, celery, radishes and cauliflower florets.

BAKED STUFFED POTATOES

(Serves 4)

Imperial (Metric)	American
4 large potatoes, weighing about 8oz (225g) each	4 large potatoes, weighing about 8 ounces each
Oil	Oil
8oz (225g) cottage or low-fat curd cheese	1 cup cottage or low-fat curd cheese
½oz (15g) butter or polyunsaturated margarine	1 tablespoon butter or polyunsaturated margarine
2 tablespoons finely chopped chives	2 tablespoons finely chopped chives
Sea salt and freshly ground black pepper	Sea salt and freshly ground black pepper
Butter or polyunsaturated margarine	Butter or polyunsaturated margarine

1. Scrub the potatoes well, then dry. With a fork prick well all over to prevent the potatoes bursting in the oven. Rub the skins with a little oil. Place on a baking sheet and bake in a preheated oven at 400°F/200°C (Gas Mark 6) for 1-1½ hours, or until soft.

2. Cut an oval piece from the top of each potato and scoop out the insides, leaving a shell about ¼ inch (6 mm) thick.

3. Mash the scooped-out potato (plus any from the lids) in a bowl with the cheese, butter, chives and seasoning to taste.

4. Spoon the mixture back into the potato shells. Put a knob of butter or margarine on each one and arrange on a baking sheet. Return the stuffed potatoes to the oven for 8-10 minutes until their tops brown and they are heated through.

YOGURT CHEESE WITH FRESH HERBS
(Serves 4)

Imperial (Metric)	American
8oz (225g) yogurt cheese	1 cup yogurt cheese
Sea salt and freshly ground black pepper	Sea salt and freshly ground black pepper
2 tablespoons single or sour cream	2 tablespoons thin or sour cream
1 clove of garlic	1 clove of garlic
2 tablespoons finely chopped chives	2 tablespoons finely chopped chives
2 tablespoons finely chopped parsley or chervil	2 tablespoons finely chopped parsley or chervil
1 tablespoon finely chopped tarragon	1 tablespoon finely chopped tarragon

1. Place the yogurt cheese into a bowl and beat until smooth, adding a little salt, pepper and the cream or sour cream.

2. Crush the garlic and stir it in with most of the chopped herbs, keeping some back to scatter over the top.

3. Pile into a small serving dish and sprinkle the remaining herbs on top. Chill for an hour or two before serving.

2.
MAIN-COURSE DISHES

CHEESE AND SPINACH FLAN

(Serves 4)

Imperial (Metric)	American
Wholemeal Pastry:	*Wholewheat Pastry:*
6 oz (175g) wholemeal flour	1½ cups wholewheat flour
Pinch of sea salt (optional)	Pinch of sea salt (optional)
3 oz (75g) butter or vegetable margarine	⅓ cup butter or vegetable margarine
Cold water to mix	Cold water to mix
Filling:	*Filling:*
1 lb (450g) fresh spinach	1 pound fresh spinach
8 oz (225g) cottage cheese, sieved	1 cup cottage cheese, sieved
2 eggs, beaten	2 eggs, beaten
4 tablespoons natural yogurt	4 tablespoons plain yogurt
Sea salt and freshly ground black pepper	Sea salt and freshly ground black pepper
Freshly grated nutmeg	Freshly grated nutmeg

1. Sift the flour and salt (if using) into a mixing bowl. Add any coarse bran left in the sieve. Rub the fat into the flour until the mixture resembles breadcrumbs. Gradually add enough water to mix to a soft dough, then turn onto a floured surface and knead lightly until smooth. Roll out thinly and use to line an 8 inch (20 cm) flan ring placed on a baking sheet. Chill for 15 minutes.

2. Meanwhile, wash and pick over the spinach. Put into a large saucepan with only the water that clings to the

leaves after washing. Cover the pan and cook over low heat for 5 minutes, or until the spinach is tender. Drain thoroughly and chop finely.

3. Mix the spinach with the cottage cheese, eggs, yogurt and season with salt, pepper and nutmeg to taste.

4. Pour the mixture into the flan case, smooth the top and bake in a preheated moderately hot oven, 375°F/190°C (Gas Mark 5) for 35-40 minutes, or until the filling is set and the top is lightly browned. Serve hot or cold with a salad.

SPINACH ROULADE WITH TOMATO SAUCE

(Serves 4-6)

Imperial (Metric)	American
For the roulade:	*For the roulade:*
1 lb (450g) fresh spinach	1 pound fresh spinach
2 oz (50g) butter or polyunsaturated margarine	¼ cup butter or polyunsaturated margarine
1½ oz (40g) plain wholemeal flour	⅓ cup plain wholewheat flour
½ pint (300 ml) milk	1⅓ cups milk
3 eggs, separated	3 eggs, separated
Sea salt and freshly ground black pepper	Sea salt and freshly ground black pepper
Freshly grated nutmeg	Freshly grated nutmeg
For the filling:	*For the filling:*
2 tablespoons vegetable oil	2 tablespoons vegetable oil
1 onion, chopped	1 onion, chopped
1 clove of garlic, peeled and crushed (optional)	1 clove of garlic, peeled and crushed (optional)
12 oz (350g) low-fat curd or cottage cheese, sieved	1½ cups low-fat curd or cottage cheese, sieved
Seasoning to taste	Seasoning to taste
To serve:	*To serve:*
½ pint (300 ml) home-made tomato sauce (page 61)	1⅓ cups home-made tomato sauce (page 61)

1. Line a 13 x 9 inch (32 x 23 cm) Swiss roll tin with greaseproof paper. Brush the paper with oil.

2. Cook the spinach in a large pan with just the water clinging to the leaves after washing, for 7 minutes or until the spinach is tender. Drain thoroughly and chop finely.

3. Melt the fat in a pan, add the flour and cook for 1-2 minutes. Gradually add the milk and bring to the boil, stirring constantly, until the sauce is thick and smooth. Remove from the heat and beat in the egg yolks, spinach, and salt, pepper and nutmeg to taste.

4. Whisk the egg whites until stiff but not dry. Using a metal spoon, fold a quarter into the spinach mixture,

then fold in the remainder. Pour the roulade mixture into the prepared tin and level the surface.

5. Bake in a preheated moderately hot oven, 400°F/200°C (Gas Mark 6) for 20 minutes, or until the roulade is well risen, firm and just beginning to turn brown.

6. Meanwhile, prepare the filling. Heat the oil in a pan, add the onion and garlic (if using) and fry until the onion is soft but not browned. Add the curd or cottage cheese and melt over gentle heat, taking care that it does not boil, or it will go stringy.

7. When the roulade is ready, turn it onto a sheet of greaseproof paper and peel off the lining paper. Spread the cheese mixture over the roulade leaving a 1 inch (2.5 cm) margin all round and carefully roll up, like a Swiss roll, using the greaseproof paper to roll it evenly. Transfer onto a warmed serving dish and pour over the hot tomato sauce to serve.

Variation: Make the roulade as directed above. Turn out onto a piece of greaseproof paper and remove the lining paper. Starting from a short edge, roll up the roulade with the paper in between and leave to cool on a wire rack. Mix the cheese with 3-4 tablespoons chopped chives or finely chopped spring onions (scallions). Carefully unroll the roulade and spread with the cheese filling. Re-roll and serve garnished with wedges of tomato and sprigs of parsley.

LENTIL CROQUETTES

(Serves 4)

Imperial (Metric)	American
6oz (175g) split red lentils	¾ cup split red lentils
1 tablespoon vegetable oil	1 tablespoon vegetable oil
1 small onion, finely chopped	1 small onion, finely chopped
¾ pint (400 ml) water	2 cups water
4oz (100g) low-fat curd cheese	½ cup low-fat curd cheese
2oz (50g) fresh wholemeal breadcrumbs	1 cup fresh wholewheat breadcrumbs
2 tablespoons chopped parsley	2 tablespoons chopped parsley
Sea salt and freshly ground black pepper	Sea salt and freshly ground black pepper
Vegetable oil for shallow frying	Vegetable oil for shallow frying

For coating:	*For coating:*
1 egg, well beaten	1 egg, well beaten
3oz (75g) fresh wholemeal breadcrumbs	1½ cups fresh wholemeal breadcrumbs

1. Pick the lentils over for stones, put them into a sieve and wash thoroughly under a running tap.

2. Heat the oil in a saucepan, add the onion and fry until transparent. Add the lentils and pour in the water. Cover the pan and bring to the boil. Reduce the heat and simmer gently, stirring occasionally, for 20-30 minutes, or until the lentils are soft and all the water has been absorbed.

3. Remove the pan from the heat and let the purée cool completely, then beat in the curd cheese, breadcrumbs, chopped parsley and salt and pepper to taste.

4. Divide the mixture into eight croquettes. Dip each one first into the beaten egg and then in the breadcrumbs to coat. Place them in the refrigerator to firm up for an hour.

5. Pour enough oil into a frying pan (skillet) to coat the base and then place over moderate heat. When hot, add the croquettes and fry until crisp and golden brown, about 5-7 minutes on each side, turning once. Drain on absorbent kitchen paper and serve hot or cold.

MUSHROOM FLAN

(Serves 4-6)

Imperial (Metric)	American
1 quantity of cream cheese pastry dough (see page 63)	1 quantity of cream cheese pastry dough (see page 63)
8 oz (225g) button mushrooms	8 ounces button mushrooms
1 oz (25g) butter or polyunsaturated margarine	2 tablespoons butter or polyunsaturated margarine
2 eggs and 1 egg yolk	2 eggs and 1 egg yolk
¼ pint (150 ml) natural yogurt	⅔ cup plain yogurt
6 tablespoons single cream	⅓ cup light cream
2 tablespoons chopped chives	2 tablespoons chopped chives
Sea salt and freshly ground black pepper	Sea salt and freshly ground black pepper

1. Roll out the pastry thinly and use to line a 9 inch (23 cm) flan ring placed on a baking sheet. Cover with a circle of greaseproof paper and baking beans. Bake the pastry blind for 15 minutes. Remove the greaseproof paper and the beans and bake for 5-10 minutes more, or until the pastry is slightly coloured.

2. Reduce the oven temperature to 375°F/190°C (Gas Mark 5).

3. Meanwhile, prepare the filling. Wipe the mushrooms and halve, quarter or leave whole, depending on size. Melt the butter or margarine in a frying pan (skillet), when hot add the mushrooms and fry for a few minutes only to seal. Remove with a slotted spoon and drain.

4. Beat the whole eggs, egg yolk, yogurt and cream together in a bowl and stir in the chopped chives, and season with salt and pepper to taste.

5. Place the drained mushrooms in the base of the flan case, pour over the custard mixture and bake for 35 minutes, or until just set and golden-brown. Serve hot or cold.

CARROT FLAN

(Serves 4)

Imperial (Metric)	American
Wholemeal Pastry:	*Wholewheat Pastry:*
4 oz (100g) wholemeal flour	1 cup wholewheat flour
Pinch of sea salt (optional)	Pinch of sea salt (optional)
2 oz (50g) butter or vegetable margarine	¼ cup butter or vegetable margarine
Cold water to mix	Cold water to mix
Filling:	*Filling:*
1 lb (450g) carrots, scrubbed and sliced	1 pound carrots, scrubbed and sliced
4 oz (100g) low-fat curd cheese	½ cup low-fat curd cheese
2 eggs, beaten	2 eggs, beaten
1 tablespoon fresh coriander, finely chopped (optional)	1 tablespoon fresh coriander, finely chopped (optional)
Sea salt and freshly ground black pepper	Sea salt and freshly ground black pepper
Freshly grated nutmeg	Freshly grated nutmeg

1. Sift the flour and salt (if using) into a bowl and add the bran from the sieve. Rub in the fat until the mixture resembles fine breadcrumbs, then add enough cold water to mix to a soft dough. Turn onto a floured surface and knead lightly until smooth. Roll out and use to line a 7 inch (18 cm) flan dish or flan ring placed on a baking sheet. Chill for 15 minutes.

2. Meanwhile prepare the filling. In a small saucepan, cook the carrots, covered, in 2 inches of boiling water for 20 minutes, or until very soft. Drain the carrots, then mash them or purée them in a food processor or blender. Place in a bowl with the curd cheese, eggs and coriander (if using), seasoning with salt, pepper and nutmeg to taste. Mix thoroughly.

3. Pour into the flan case, smooth the top and bake in a preheated moderate oven 350°F/180°C (Gas Mark 4) for 30-45 minutes, or until the pastry is cooked and the filling set.

LEEK FLAN

(Serves 4-6)

Imperial (Metric)	American
6oz (175g) wholemeal shortcrust pastry (page 40)	6 ounces wholewheat shortcrust pastry (page 40)
½oz (15g) butter or margarine	1 tablespoon butter or margarine
1 lb (450g) leeks, cleaned, trimmed and sliced	1 pound leeks, cleaned, trimmed and sliced
2 eggs	2 eggs
¼ pint (150 ml) milk	⅔ cup milk
4oz (100g) low-fat curd cheese	½ cup low-fat curd cheese
Sea salt and freshly ground black pepper	Sea salt and freshly ground black pepper
Freshly grated nutmeg	Freshly grated nutmeg
1½oz (40g) vegetarian Cheddar cheese, grated	⅓ cup vegetarian Cheddar cheese, grated

1. Roll out the pastry on a lightly floured surface and use to line an 8 inch (20 cm) flan ring placed on a baking sheet. Lightly prick the base with a fork and line with greaseproof paper and baking beans kept for the purpose.

2. Bake on the centre shelf of a preheated moderately hot oven, 400°F/200°C (Gas Mark 6) for 15 minutes. Remove the greaseproof paper and the beans and bake for 5 minutes more. Remove the flan and reduce the oven temperature to 375°F/190°C (Gas Mark 5).

3. Melt the butter or margarine in a saucepan. Add the leeks, cover the pan and cook over a very low heat, stirring occasionally, for 10 minutes, or until the leeks are tender. Using a slotted spoon, transfer the leeks to the flan case.

4. Beat together the eggs, milk, cheese, salt, pepper and nutmeg to taste. Pour into the flan case, sprinkle with the grated cheese, then return the flan to the oven and bake for 25-30 minutes, or until the filling is set and lightly browned on top.

BOILED POTATOES WITH COTTAGE OR CURD CHEESE

(Serves 4)

Imperial (Metric)	American
1½lbs (680g) new potatoes	1½ pounds new potatoes
1 sprig of mint	1 sprig of mint
1½oz (40g) butter or vegetable margarine	3 tablespoons butter or vegetable margarine
Sea salt and freshly ground black pepper	Sea salt and freshly ground black pepper
6oz (175g) cottage or low-fat curd cheese	¾ cup cottage or low-fat curd cheese

1. Place potatoes in a saucepan and add sufficient water so that the potatoes will just be covered. Add the sprig of mint and bring to the boil.

2. Scrub the potatoes or scrape them if preferred, and cook gently in the boiling water for 20 minutes or until tender. Strain the potatoes through a colander, place them over an empty hot saucepan and cover with crumpled clean cloth to keep them warm and dry. Peel if desired.

3. Melt the butter or margarine in a saucepan, add the potatoes and shake over gentle heat until well coated. Season with salt and pepper to taste. Put them into a hot serving dish. Crumble or sieve the cheese over the potatoes and serve.

COTTAGE CHEESE AND CUCUMBER MOUSSE

(Serves 6)

Imperial (Metric)	American
12oz (350g) cottage cheese	1½ cups cottage cheese
4oz (100g) cream cheese	½ cup cream cheese
¾ medium cucumber, peeled and diced small	¾ medium cucumber, peeled and diced small
1 tablespoon chopped parsley	1 tablespoon chopped parsley
1 tablespoon chopped chives	1 tablespoon chopped chives
1 tablespoon chopped thyme	1 tablespoon chopped thyme
1 tablespoon cider vinegar	1 tablespoon cider vinegar
Sea salt	Sea salt
½ pint (300 ml) vegetable stock	1⅓ cups vegetable stock
¼oz (7g) agar-agar	2 rounded teaspoons agar-agar
3 egg whites	3 egg whites

To garnish: — *To garnish:*

¼ cucumber, unpeeled and thinly sliced	¼ cucumber, unpeeled and thinly sliced
Sprigs of watercress	Sprigs of watercress

1. Press the cottage cheese through a sieve. Mix with the cream cheese. Stir in the chopped cucumber, herbs, vinegar and salt to taste.

2. Bring the vegetable stock to the boil, sprinkle on the agar-agar and boil for 2 minutes, stirring briskly to dissolve the lumps. Leave to cool slightly then add to the cheese mixture.

3. Whisk the egg whites with a pinch of salt until stiff and fold into the cheese mixture.

4. Pour the mixture into a lightly oiled decorative mould and leave to set in the refrigerator. Turn out onto a serving dish and garnish with cucumber slices and watercress to serve.

LEEK AND POTATO BAKE

(Serves 4-6)

Imperial (Metric)	American
1 lb (450g) leeks, trimmed, washed and cut into ½ inch (1 cm) rings	1 pound leeks, trimmed, washed and cut into ½ inch thick rings
2 lbs (900g) potatoes, peeled and cubed	2 pounds potatoes, peeled and cubed
1 large onion, peeled and sliced	1 large onion, peeled and sliced
¼ pint(150 ml) water	⅔ cup water
1 dessertspoon yeast extract	2 teaspoons yeast extract

For the topping:

For the topping:

Imperial (Metric)	American
4 oz (100g) low-fat curd cheese	½ cup low-fat curd cheese
2 oz (50g) butter or vegetable margarine	¼ cup butter or vegetable margarine
2 level teaspoons made-mustard	2 level teaspoons made-mustard
3 oz (75g) jumbo or rolled oats	1 cup jumbo or rolled oats
2 fl oz (60 ml) milk	¼ cup milk
Sea salt and freshly ground black pepper	Sea salt and freshly ground black pepper

1. Place the leeks, potatoes, onion, water and yeast extract in a saucepan. Cover, bring to the boil and cook for 8 minutes, stirring occasionally. Taste and adjust the seasoning.

2. Meanwhile, make the topping. Place the curd cheese and butter in a bowl and beat with a wooden spoon to soften. Stir in the mustard, oats and milk. Season with sea salt and freshly ground black pepper.

3. Pour the vegetables and liquid into a 3 pint (1.75 litre) ovenproof dish. Spoon the topping over and cook in a preheated moderate oven, 350°F/180°C (Gas Mark 4) for 45 minutes to one hour. Serve immediately.

SPAGHETTI WITH RICOTTA SAUCE

(Serves 4)

Imperial (Metric)	American
Sea salt	Sea salt
10oz (275g) wholemeal spaghetti	10 ounces wholewheat spaghetti
6oz (175g) Ricotta cheese	¾ cup Ricotta cheese
2oz (50g) grated Pecorino cheese	½ cup grated Pecorino cheese
Pinch of freshly grated nutmeg	Pinch of freshly grated nutmeg
Freshly ground black pepper	Freshly ground black pepper
2 tablespoons chopped parsley	2 tablespoons chopped parsley
½oz (15g) butter	1 tablespoon butter

1. Bring a large pan of water to a rapid boil (add salt when boiling). Lower ends of the spaghetti into the water, pressing them in further around the side of the pan as the ends soften. Boil uncovered for about 10 minutes, or until *al dente*, firm to the bite.

2. While the pasta is cooking, beat the Ricotta with a wooden spoon until very smooth; add the grated Pecorino cheese, nutmeg, and seasoning to taste. Mix in the parsley.

3. Drain the spaghetti and return to the pan. Add the butter and Ricotta sauce and toss together over a low heat for a few seconds. Serve immediately with extra Pecorino cheese passed around separately, if you wish.

AUBERGINE (EGGPLANT) CHEESE BAKE

(Serves 4)

Imperial (Metric)	American
1½lbs (750g) aubergines	1½ pounds eggplants
Sea salt	Sea salt
Vegetable oil for frying	Vegetable oil for frying
1 small onion, finely chopped	1 small onion, finely chopped
1 clove of garlic, peeled and crushed	1 clove of garlic, peeled and crushed
1 lb (450g) fresh tomatoes, skinned, seeded and coarsely chopped	1 pound fresh tomatoes, skinned, seeded and coarsely chopped
4oz (100g) Ricotta cheese	½ cup Ricotta cheese
1 egg	1 egg
2oz (50g) freshly grated Parmesan cheese (or Pecorino)	½ cup freshly grated Parmesan cheese (or Pecorino)
¼ pint (150 ml) double cream or natural yogurt	⅔ cup heavy cream or natural yogurt
2 tablespoons chopped basil leaves	2 tablespoons chopped basil leaves
Freshly ground black pepper	Freshly ground black pepper

1. Remove stalks from the aubergines (eggplants) and cut lengthways into ¼ inch (6 mm) thick slices. Put them into a colander, sprinkle lightly with salt, then leave to stand for 1 hour.

2. Heat 2 tablespoons of oil in a small frying pan (skillet), add the onion and garlic and fry until soft but not brown. Add the tomatoes, salt lightly and simmer, uncovered, for 15-20 minutes, or until most of the liquid has evaporated and the tomatoes have reduced to a thick purée.

3. Meanwhile, rinse the aubergine (eggplant) slices under cold running water, then drain and pat dry with absorbent kitchen paper.

4. Cover the base of a large frying pan (skillet) with a thin layer of oil. When the oil is very hot, add the aubergine (eggplant) slices in batches and fry briskly until browned on both sides. (They will absorb the oil quite quickly,

so keep adding more oil as needed). Drain on absorbent kitchen paper and keep warm.

5. Place the Ricotta cheese in a bowl with the egg and beat with a whisk until smooth. Stir in enough Parmesan to form a thick paste, then gradually add cream until the mixture has a thick pouring consistency. Season to taste.

6. Put half of the aubergine (eggplant) slices in the bottom of an ovenproof dish. Cover with the tomato mixture, add the chopped basil leaves and season with freshly ground black pepper. Arrange the rest of the aubergine (eggplant) slices on top, then pour over the cheese and cream mixture.

7. Sprinkle the remaining Parmesan over the top and bake in a very hot oven preheated to 450°F/230°C (Gas Mark 8) for 10 minutes, then lower the heat to 375°F/190°C (Gas Mark 5) for a further 25 minutes, or until the surface is golden brown. Serve immediately as a main dish.

COURGETTES (ZUCCHINI) BAKED WITH CHEESE

(Serves 4)

Imperial (Metric)	American
1¾lbs (750g) courgettes	1¾ pounds zucchini
Oil for frying	Oil for frying
1 small onion, peeled and chopped	1 small onion, peeled and chopped
1 clove of garlic, peeled and crushed	1 clove of garlic, peeled and crushed
14oz (400g) tin tomatoes or 1lb (450g) fresh tomatoes, skinned, chopped and seeded	1 medium can tomatoes or 1 pound fresh tomatoes, skinned, chopped and seeded
1 tablespoon chopped basil or ½ teaspoon dried	1 tablespoon chopped basil or ½ teaspoon dried
Sea salt and freshly ground black pepper	Sea salt and freshly ground black pepper
8oz (225g) low-fat curd, Ricotta or cottage cheese	1 cup low-fat curd, Ricotta or cottage cheese
1oz (25g) grated Pecorino cheese	¼ cup grated Pecorino cheese

1. Trim the courgettes (zucchini) then thickly slice them widthways.

2. Cover the base of a large frying pan (skillet) with a thin layer of oil. Place over moderate heat and fry the courgette (zucchini) slices in batches until golden brown on both sides. Drain on absorbent kitchen paper and keep warm.

3. Heat 2 tablespoons of oil in a heavy pan, add the onion and fry until softened, then add the garlic, tomatoes and basil. Add a little salt and pepper and stir with a wooden spoon to break up the tomatoes. Cover and simmer gently for 20 minutes, stirring occasionally.

4. Arrange a third of the courgette (zucchini) slices in an ovenproof dish. Cover with half of the tomato mixture, then top with half of the cheese. Repeat the layers, finishing with the courgette (zucchini) slices. Sprinkle with the Pecorino and bake in a preheated moderate oven, 350°F/180°C (Gas Mark 4), for 25 to 30 minutes.

Variation: Aubergine (eggplant) may be used in place of the courgettes (zucchini).

STUFFED COURGETTES

(Serves 4-6)

Imperial (Metric)	American
6 plump courgettes, about 6 inches (15 cm) long	6 plump zucchini, about 6 inches long
Sea salt	Sea salt
4oz (100g) Ricotta or low-fat curd cheese	½ cup Ricotta or low-fat curd cheese
4oz (100g) fresh wholemeal breadcrumbs	breadcrumbs
4 tablespoons flaked almonds	4 tablespoons slivered almonds
Rind and juice of ½ lemon	Rind and juice of ½ lemon
Freshly ground black pepper	Freshly ground black pepper

1. Parboil the courgettes (zucchini) in boiling salted water for 5 minutes; drain. Cut in half lengthways, then scoop out and finely chop the centres.

2. Mix together the cheese, breadcrumbs, flaked (slivered) almonds, scooped-out courgette (zucchini) centres, lemon juice and rind. Add salt and pepper to taste.

3. Divide the mixture between the courgette (zucchini) 'boats' and arrange side by side in a well oiled shallow ovenproof dish. Bake in a preheated oven at 350°F/190°C (Gas Mark 5) for 35-40 minutes.

SPINACH BAKE

(Serves 4)

Imperial (Metric)	American
1 lb (450g) fresh spinach	1 pound fresh spinach
8 oz (225g) low-fat curd, cottage or Ricotta cheese	1 cup low-fat curd, cottage or Ricotta Cheese
2 eggs, separated	2 eggs, separated
Sea salt and freshly ground black pepper	Sea salt and freshly ground black pepper
Freshly grated nutmeg	Freshly grated nutmeg
1 oz (25g) freshly grated Parmesan or Pecorino cheese	¼ cup freshly grated Parmesan or Pecorino cheese

1. Cook the spinach in a large pan with just the water clinging to the leaves after washing, for 5 minutes or until tender. Drain thoroughly and chop finely.

2. Place in a bowl with the cheese, egg yolks, salt, pepper and nutmeg to taste; mix well. Whisk the egg whites until stiff and fold into the mixture.

3. Turn into 4 individual buttered 'gratin' dishes or a large ovenproof dish. Sprinkle with the grated Parmesan cheese and bake in a preheated oven at 350°F/180°C (Gas Mark 4) for 20 minutes. Serve at once.

SCALLOPED POTATOES WITH COTTAGE CHEESE AND ONION

(Serves 4)

Imperial (Metric)	American
1½lbs (680g) potatoes	1½ pounds potatoes
1 small onion	1 small onion
6-8oz (175-225g) cottage cheese	¾-1 cup cottage cheese
2oz (50g) butter or vegetable margarine, melted	¼ cup butter or vegetable margarine, melted
Sea salt and freshly ground black pepper	Sea salt and freshly ground black pepper
¼ pint (150ml) natural yogurt	⅔ cup plain yogurt
1 egg	1 egg

1. Peel and thinly slice the potatoes. Peel and finely chop the onion.

2. Mix the cottage cheese and melted fat together, adding salt and pepper to taste.

3. Grease a 2½ pint (1.5 litre) ovenproof dish. Arrange a layer of the potatoes on the bottom of the dish, season lightly with salt and pepper, then sprinkle over some of the cheese and add a little chopped onion. Repeat the layers, ending with the top layer of potatoes attractively arranged in overlapping circles. Cover and bake in an oven preheated to 375°F/190°C (Gas Mark 5) for 1 hour or until the potatoes are tender.

4. In a small bowl, beat together the yogurt and egg, pour on top of the potatoes and bake uncovered for 30 minutes more, or until the potatoes are cooked and the top is crisp and brown. Serve hot.

ARTICHOKE BAKE

(Serves 4)

Imperial (Metric)	American
4 medium-sized globe artichokes	4 medium-sized globe artichokes
1 lemon cut in half	1 lemon cut in half
Sea salt	Sea salt
8oz (225g) Ricotta cheese	1 cup Ricotta cheese
1oz (25g) freshly grated Parmesan or Pecorino cheese	¼ cup freshly grated Parmesan or Pecorino cheese
3 eggs	3 eggs
3 tablespoons milk	3 tablespoons milk
Freshly ground black pepper	Freshly ground black pepper
Wholemeal breadcrumbs (optional)	Wholewheat breadcrumbs (optional)

1. Break the stems off the artichokes and strip off the hard outer leaves; using a sharp knife, cut off and discard two-thirds of the tops so that only the tender part is left. Cut the artichokes in half (from top to bottom) and remove the chokes. As soon as you have trimmed each of the artichokes, rub the surface with half the lemon and then plunge it into a bowl of cold water acidulated with the juice of the other half of the lemon (this is to stop the artichokes turning black).

2. Boil the washed and trimmed artichokes in lightly salted water for 15 minutes. Drain, allow to cool, then cut lengthwise into thin slices. Put them into a buttered ovenproof dish.

3. Place the Ricotta cheese in a bowl with the Parmesan, eggs, milk, salt and pepper. Beat the ingredients together until well blended, then pour over the artichokes and, if you like, sprinkle breadcrumbs or more grated Parmesan cheese over the top. Bake in a pre-heated oven, 350°F/180°C (Gas Mark 4) for about 20 minutes, or until the artichokes are tender. Serve immediately.

PURÉED POTATOES WITH CHEESE

(Serves 4)

Imperial (Metric)	American
2 lb (900g) floury potatoes	2 pounds floury potatoes
2 oz (50g) butter or vegetable margarine	¼ cup butter or vegetable margarine
¼ pint (150 ml) single cream	⅔ cup light cream
6-8oz (175-225g) fresh cottage cheese	¾-1 cup fresh cottage cheese
1 clove of garlic, peeled and crushed	1 clove of garlic, peeled and crushed
Sea salt and freshly ground black pepper	Sea salt and freshly ground black pepper
2 tablespoons chopped parsley to garnish	2 tablespoons chopped parsley to garnish

1. Scrub the potatoes, boil in their skins until tender, about 20 minutes. Drain well. Peel, then pass them through a sieve or mash well.

2. Heat the butter and cream in a large, heavy-based pan until the butter is melted. Blend the potatoes into the hot cream, then add the cheese and garlic, stirring the mixture over a low heat until well combined and the purée heated through. Season to taste. Turn into a hot serving dish, sprinkle with chopped parsley, and serve immediately.

MUSHROOM AND VEGETABLE BAKE

(Serves 4-6)

Imperial (Metric)	American
2 oz (50g) butter or vegetable margarine	¼ cup butter or vegetable margarine
1 large onion, finely chopped	1 large onion, finely chopped
¾ lb (350g) courgettes, wiped and sliced	¾ pound zucchini, wiped and sliced
8 oz (225g) mushrooms, wiped and sliced	1½ cups mushrooms, wiped and sliced
6 oz (175g) fresh wholemeal breadcrumbs	3 cups fresh wholewheat breadcrumbs
8 oz (225g) cottage cheese	1 cup cottage cheese
4 oz (100g) mixed nuts, coarsely chopped	¾ cup mixed nuts, coarsely chopped
1 large teaspoon mixed dried herbs (or 1 tablespoon fresh)	1 large teaspoon mixed dried herbs (or 1 tablespoon fresh)
2 level tablespoons tomato purée	2 level tablespoons tomato paste
4 oz (100g) cream cheese	½ cup cream cheese
Sea salt and freshly ground black pepper	Sea salt and freshly ground black pepper

1. Melt the butter or margarine in a large frying pan (skillet). Add the onion and courgettes (zucchini) and fry until the onion is transparent. Add the mushrooms and continue to cook for 1-2 minutes.

2. In a large mixing bowl, combine the vegetable mixture with all the remaining ingredients, seasoning with salt and pepper to taste. Mix thoroughly.

3. Turn the mixture into an ovenproof dish. Cover with foil and bake in a preheated oven, 375°F/190°C (Gas Mark 5) for 40 minutes. 10 minutes before the end of the cooking time remove the foil to brown the surface.

RAVIOLI WITH RICOTTA AND SPINACH FILLING

(Serves 4)

Imperial (Metric)	American
For the pasta dough:	*For the pasta dough:*
8oz (225g) plain wholemeal flour	2 cups plain wholewheat flour
Pinch of sea salt	Pinch of sea salt
2 eggs	2 eggs
1 tablespoon olive oil	1 tablespoon olive oil
A little cold water	A little cold water
For the filling:	*For the filling:*
6oz (175g) fresh spinach	6 ounces fresh spinach
6oz (175g) Ricotta or low-fat curd cheese	¾ cup Ricotta or low-fat curd cheese
2oz (50g) grated Parmesan cheese	½ cup grated Parmesan cheese
2 teaspoons grated onion	2 teaspoons grated onion
1 egg, beaten	1 egg, beaten
Sea salt and freshly ground black pepper	Sea salt and freshly ground black pepper
Freshly grated nutmeg	Freshly grated nutmeg
For the tomato sauce:	*For the tomato sauce:*
2 x 14oz (400g) tins tomatoes	2 medium cans tomatoes
1oz (25g) butter	2 tablespoons butter
1 tablespoon olive oil	1 tablespoon olive oil
1 large clove garlic, peeled and crushed	1 large clove garlic, peeled and crushed
1 level tablespoon tomato purée	1 level tablespoon tomato paste
1 tablespoon chopped fresh basil or ½ teaspoon dried	1 tablespoon chopped fresh basil or ½ teaspoon dried
Sea salt and freshly ground black pepper	Sea salt and freshly ground black pepper
2 tablespoons fresh parsley, chopped	2 tablespoons fresh parsley, chopped

1. Sift the flour and salt into a large mixing bowl, or in a mound on a clean work surface, and add the bran that remains in the sieve. Make a well in the centre. Lightly beat the eggs and oil together and pour into the well. With a fork, gradually draw the flour into the egg mixture until as much flour as possible is absorbed.

Using your hands, work in the remaining flour, adding a few drops of water as you do so to make a firm but pliable dough.

2. On a well-floured surface knead the dough, using the heel of the hand. Continue kneading for 5 to 10 minutes or until the dough is smooth, elastic and slightly shiny. Shape it into a ball and leave to rest for 10 to 20 minutes on a lightly-floured surface covered with a bowl or damp cloth.

3. While the dough is resting prepare the ravioli filling. Cook the spinach in a large pan, with just the water clinging to the leaves after washing and a pinch of salt, for 5 minutes; drain thoroughly. Chop finely and put in a bowl. Add the two cheeses, onion, egg, and salt, pepper and nutmeg to taste; mix thoroughly. Set aside.

4. Put the pasta on a lightly-floured surface and divide it into two. Pat out to a rectangle, then roll out evenly to 1/16 inch (2mm) thickness sheet of pasta. If pasta sticks, ease it carefully and flour lightly underneath. Make sure there are no holes or creases. Cover with a clean damp cloth and repeat with the other half of the dough.

5. Place teaspoonfuls of the filling evenly spaced at 2 inch (5 cm) intervals across and down the sheet of dough that has just been rolled out. With a pastry brush dipped in cold water, damp the spaces between the filling to help seal the ravioli later.

6. Uncover the other sheet of pasta, carefully lift this on the rolling pin to avoid stretching and unroll it over the first sheet, easing gently. Press down firmly around the pockets of filling and along the dampened lines to push out any trapped air and seal well.

7. With a special ravioli cutter, serrated-edged pastry wheel or even a sharp knife, cut the ravioli into squares between the pouches. Place the ravioli in a single layer on greaseproof paper or a floured tray, and leave to dry for about 30 minutes before cooking.

8. Meanwhile prepare the sauce. Push the tomatoes, with their liquid, through a sieve. Heat the butter and oil in a

pan, add the garlic and cook for 1 minute. Add the tomato purée (paste), basil and season with salt and pepper to taste. Bring to the boil; reduce heat, simmer uncovered for 30 minutes or until sauce is reduced by about half. Stir in the parsley.

9. Cook the ravioli, a few at a time, in a large pan of boiling salted water, with 1-2 tablespoons of oil, for 5-8 minutes until *al dente* (tender, but firm to the bite). Remove with a slotted spoon, drain thoroughly, and keep them warm whilst you cook the rest. Pour the hot tomato sauce over and serve with grated cheese.

CREAM CHEESE PASTRY DOUGH

Imperial (Metric)	American
3 oz (75g) cream cheese	⅓ cup cream cheese
4 oz (100g) butter, softened	½ cup butter, softened
6 oz (175g) wholemeal flour	1½ cups wholewheat flour

1. Blend the cream cheese and butter thoroughly. Sift the flour into the cheese mixture and add the bran from the sieve. Work in well, binding the ingredients together to form a soft dough, without the addition of liquid.

2. Wrap in cling film and chill in the refrigerator for at least one hour before using.

Note: This is enough dough for an 8 inch (20 cm) pie tin or 24 tartlet moulds.

3.
SALADS AND
SALAD DRESSINGS

STUFFED LETTUCE

(Serves 4)

Imperial (Metric)	American
1 Iceberg lettuce	1 Iceberg lettuce
8oz (225g) cottage cheese	1 cup cottage cheese
4oz (100g) blue cheese of your choice, diced	⅔ cup blue cheese of your choice, diced
2 tablespoons mayonnaise or cream	2 tablespoons mayonnaise or cream
1oz (25g) chopped walnuts	¼ cup chopped English walnuts
4oz (100g) black grapes, halved and deseeded	4 ounces black grapes, halved and deseeded
Sea salt and freshly ground black pepper	Sea salt and freshly ground black pepper

1. Cut the top off the lettuce and scoop out the centre, leaving a thin shell. Shred the centre and lid; set aside.

2. In a bowl, combine together the cheeses, mayonnaise or cream, walnuts, grapes and one-third of the chopped centre of lettuce, seasoning with salt and pepper to taste; pack the lettuce cavity with this. Chill lightly and serve, garnished with remaining shredded lettuce.

TOMATO AND WATERCRESS SALAD

(Serves 4)

Imperial (Metric)	American
1 bunch of watercress, washed and trimmed	1 bunch of watercress, washed and trimmed
4 large firm, ripe tomatoes	4 large firm, ripe tomatoes
8oz (225g) acid curd cheese	1 cup acid curd cheese
4 tablespoons finely chopped chives	4 tablespoons finely chopped chives
¼ teaspoon mustard	¼ teaspoon mustard
1 tablespoon white wine vinegar	1 tablespoon white wine vinegar
3 tablespoons olive oil	3 tablespoons olive oil
Sea salt and freshly ground black pepper	Sea salt and freshly ground black pepper

1. Line four individual plates with the watercress.

2. Wipe the tomatoes and slice them thinly, then arrange neatly in the centre of the watercress.

3. Divide the curd cheese into four and shape into balls, flatten them slightly, then roll each one in the chopped chives. Place them on top of the tomatoes.

4. In a small bowl, mix together the mustard, vinegar, oil and seasoning. Serve the dressing separately, or pour over each plate just before serving.

COTTAGE CHEESE AND SLICED PINEAPPLE SALAD

(Serves 4)

Imperial (Metric)
12oz (350g) cottage cheese
2 tablespoons finely
   chopped chives
1 tablespoon mayonnaise
2oz (50g) cashew nuts,
   toasted and coarsely
   chopped
Sea salt and freshly ground
   black pepper
8 lettuce leaves
4 slices of fresh or canned
   pineapple (with no added
   sugar)
Paprika

American
1½ cups cottage cheese
2 tablespoons finely
   chopped chives
1 tablespoon mayonnaise
½ cup cashew nuts, toasted
   and coarsely chopped
Sea salt and freshly ground
   black pepper
8 lettuce leaves
4 slices of fresh or canned
   pineapple (with no added
   sugar)
Paprika

To garnish:

A few black olives
8 small sprigs of watercress

To garnish:

A few black olives
8 small sprigs of watercress

1. Mix the cottage cheese with the chives, mayonnaise, cashews and salt and pepper to taste.

2. Arrange the lettuce leaves on four individual serving plates. Place a pineapple slice on top, then pile the mixture in the centre.

3. Sprinkle with paprika. Garnish each portion with black olives and the sprigs of watercress.

CREAM CHEESE COLESLAW

(Serves 4-6)

Imperial (Metric)	American
12oz (350g) hard white cabbage	¾ pound hard white cabbage
2 small red-skinned eating apples or Cox's	2 small red-skinned eating apples or Cox's
4 spring onions, chopped	4 scallions, chopped
2 sticks of celery, chopped	2 celery stalks, chopped
4oz (100g) cream cheese	½ cup cream cheese
4 tablespoons mayonnaise	¼ cup mayonnaise
1 tablespoon lemon juice	1 tablespoon lemon juice
Sea salt and freshly ground black pepper	Sea salt and freshly ground black pepper
2 tablespoons roasted sunflower seeds	2 tablespoons roasted sunflower seeds

1. Discard the coarse outer leaves and thick stalk from the cabbage. Shred the cabbage finely and place in a bowl.

2. Wipe and cut the apples into quarters. Remove cores, chop and add to the bowl with the spring onions (scallions) and celery.

3. To make the dressing, beat the cheese with the mayonnaise, lemon juice, salt and pepper. Mix well, until free of lumps.

4. Pour the dressing over the salad and toss well. Serve immediately, sprinkled with the sunflower seeds.

CHEESE-STUFFED TOMATO SALAD

(Serves 4 or 8)

These stuffed tomatoes are useful for hors d'oeuvre or for a salad, garnished with any kind of vegetables.

Imperial (Metric)	American
8 large, firm tomatoes	8 large, firm tomatoes
8oz (225g) cottage cheese	1 cup cottage cheese
3 inches (8 cm) cucumber, finely chopped	3 inches cucumber, finely chopped
1 bunch of watercress, washed, trimmed and finely chopped	1 bunch of watercress, washed, trimmed and finely chopped
1 tablespoon finely chopped chives	1 tablespoon finely chopped chives
Sea salt and freshly ground black pepper	Sea salt and freshly ground black pepper
A few lettuce leaves	A few lettuce leaves

To garnish:	*To garnish:*
Selection of raw vegetables (carrot sticks, radish 'roses', chicory leaves)	Selection of raw vegetables (carrot sticks, radish 'roses', endive leaves)

1. Cut a circle around the bottom of each tomato. Lift off 'lid' and carefully scoop out the pulp into a bowl. Leave the tomato shells upside down to drain on kitchen paper for 15 minutes.

2. Mix the chopped tomato pulp, cottage cheese, cucumber, watercress and chives together. Season with salt and pepper to taste.

3. Spoon the filling into the tomato shells until they are quite full and almost overflowing, then replace the lids at a slight angle.

4. Line a flat serving dish or large plate with the lettuce leaves. Place the stuffed tomatoes on top and arrange the prepared vegetables around the outside. Serve with mayonnaise.

STUFFED PEACH SALAD

(Serves 4)

Imperial (Metric)	American
4 large ripe peaches, peeled, halved and stoned	4 large ripe peaches, peeled, halved and stoned
Juice of ½ lemon	Juice of ½ lemon
8 oz (225g) cottage or low-fat curd cheese	1 cup cottage or low-fat curd cheese
2 oz (50g) chopped walnuts	½ cup chopped English walnuts
8 lettuce leaves	8 lettuce leaves

1. Place the peaches in a mixing bowl and sprinkle with the lemon juice. Toss until well coated in the juice.

2. In a separate bowl, mix together the cottage cheese and walnuts.

3. Arrange the lettuce leaves on four individual serving plates. Place two peach halves on top, cut side up. Spoon the cottage cheese mixture into the peach halves and serve.

CARROT AND CURD CHEESE LETTUCE PARCELS

(Serves 6-8)

Imperial (Metric)
1 round lettuce, washed
8 oz (225g) low-fat curd cheese
1 large carrot, finely grated
2 tablespoons mayonnaise,
  preferably home-made
Sea salt and freshly ground
  black pepper

Dressing:

¼ pint (150 ml) olive oil
4 tablespoons cider or wine
  vinegar
½ level teaspoon mustard
  powder
¼ level teaspoon raw cane
  sugar (optional)
1 tablespoon fresh parsley,
  chopped
Sea salt and freshly ground
  black pepper

American
1 round lettuce, washed
1 cup low-fat curd cheese
1 large carrot, finely grated
2 tablespoons mayonnaise,
  preferably home-made
Sea salt and freshly ground
  black pepper

Dressing:

⅔ cup olive oil
4 tablespoons cider or wine
  vinegar
½ level teaspoon mustard
  powder
¼ level teaspoon raw cane
  sugar (optional)
1 tablespoon fresh parsley,
  chopped
Sea salt and freshly ground
  black pepper

1. Dry the lettuce leaves on kitchen paper.

2. In a bowl combine the cheese, grated carrot, mayonnaise and seasoning together until evenly mixed.

3. Place a little of the mixture towards the stalk end of each lettuce leaf, fold the sides of each leaf into the centre and then roll up to make neat parcels. Arrange with the loose ends tucked underneath in a serving dish.

4. Place all the dressing ingredients in a bottle with a screw-top. Shake bottle vigorously until contents are well blended and pour over parcels just before serving.

COTTAGE CHEESE, TOMATO AND ORANGE SALAD

(Serves 2)

Imperial (Metric)	American
2 medium oranges	2 medium oranges
1 small green pepper	1 small green pepper
8oz (225g) cottage cheese	1 cup cottage cheese
Sea salt and freshly ground black pepper	Sea salt and freshly ground black pepper
2 large tomatoes	2 large tomatoes
1 tablespoon fresh parsley, chopped	1 tablespoon fresh parsley, chopped

1. Hold the oranges over a serving dish and cut off peel and white pith with a small sharp or serrated knife. Cut down between each segment to release flesh.

2. Cut the pepper in half lengthwise, remove stalk, seeds and white pith. Cut the pepper into thin strips.

3. Mix the cottage cheese with the pepper. Season with salt and pepper to taste.

4. Wipe tomatoes, cut into thick wedges.

5. Arrange the orange segments and the tomato wedges alternately round the edge of a serving dish. Pile the cottage cheese and pepper in the centre. Garnish with parsley.

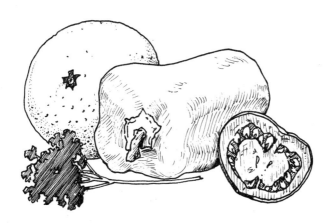

STUFFED PEPPER SALAD

(Serves 4)

Imperial (Metric)	American
6oz (175g) medium-fat curd cheese	¾ cup medium-fat curd cheese
1 tablespoon finely chopped chives	1 tablespoon finely chopped chives
1 tablespoon chopped parsley	1 tablespoon chopped parsley
1 teaspoon vegetarian Worcester sauce	1 teaspoon vegetarian Worcester sauce
Sea salt and freshly ground black pepper	Sea salt and freshly ground black pepper
1 medium-sized red pepper	1 medium-sized red pepper
1 medium-sized green pepper	1 medium-sized green pepper
8oz (225g) button mushrooms	8 ounces button mushrooms
A few crisp lettuce leaves	A few crisp lettuce leaves
Sprigs of parsley to garnish	Sprigs of parsley to garnish

1. Place the cheese in a mixing bowl. Blend in the chives, parsley, Worcester sauce, and salt and pepper to taste.

2. Wipe the peppers, cut a thin slice from the stalk end of each and remove the seeds and white pith.

3. Wipe and chop the mushrooms, stir into the cheese mixture. Fill the cavity of each pepper with the cheese and mushroom filling, pressing it in gently with the back of a metal spoon. Wrap each pepper in cling film (plastic wrap) and place in the refrigerator for at least 30 minutes.

4. Slice each pepper thinly and arrange the rings of red and green pepper alternately on a serving dish lined with lettuce leaves; garnish with sprigs of parsley.

CALIFORNIAN FRUIT SALAD WITH COTTAGE CHEESE DRESSING

(Serves 4)

Imperial (Metric)	American
1 crisp lettuce, preferably Iceberg	1 crisp lettuce, preferably Iceberg
Juice of 1 orange	Juice of 1 orange
2 red skinned eating apples, cored, sliced and sprinkled with lemon juice	2 red skinned eating apples, cored, sliced and sprinkled with lemon juice
2 oranges, peeled and segmented	2 oranges, peeled and segmented
1 pear, cored and sliced	1 pear, cored and sliced
1 kiwi fruit, peeled and sliced	1 kiwi fruit, peeled and sliced
4oz (100g) pineapple, cubed	4 ounces pineapple, cubed
½lb (225g) hulled strawberries or other fruit in season	½ pound hulled strawberries or other fruit in season
1 quantity cottage cheese dressing (see page 74)	1 quantity cottage cheese dressing (see page 74)
2oz (50g) flaked almonds (toasted)	½ cup slivered almonds (toasted)

1. Shred or tear the lettuce into bite-sized pieces, place in a bowl with the orange juice and sliced fruit.

2. Pour the cottage cheese dressing over the salad and sprinkle with the toasted almonds to serve.

COTTAGE CHEESE DRESSING I

Imperial (Metric)
8oz (225g) cottage cheese
¼ pint (150 ml) buttermilk
2 tablespoons wine vinegar
Sea salt and freshly ground
    black pepper

American
1 cup cottage cheese
⅔ cup buttermilk
2 tablespoons wine vinegar
Sea salt and freshly ground
    black pepper

1. Whisk all the ingredients in a blender until smooth.

COTTAGE CHEESE DRESSING II

Imperial (Metric)
4oz (100g) cottage cheese
2 tablespoons cider vinegar
3 tablespoons French
    dressing
1 small clove of garlic, peeled
    and crushed

American
½ cup cottage cheese
2 tablespoons cider vinegar
3 tablespoons French
    dressing
1 small clove of garlic, peeled
    and crushed

1. Mix together all the ingredients, and beat until smooth.

CREAM CHEESE DRESSING

(To use instead of mayonnaise)

Imperial (Metric)
4oz (100g) cream cheese
¼ pint (150 ml) olive oil
2 tablespoons lemon juice
Sea salt and freshly ground
    black pepper
1 tablespoon fresh herbs
    (optional)

American
½ cup cream cheese
⅔ cup olive oil
2 tablespoons lemon juice
Sea salt and freshly ground
    black pepper
1 tablespoon fresh herbs
    (optional)

1. Put the cream cheese in a bowl. Gradually add the oil,
   beating well between each addition. A small balloon
   whisk is ideal for this. Beat in the lemon juice, add salt,
   pepper and herbs, if used. Alternatively, place all the
   ingredients except for the herbs in a blender or food
   processor, and process until smooth. Cover and store
   in the refrigerator until required.

CURD CHEESE AND YOGURT DRESSING

Imperial (Metric)	American
4 oz (100g) low-fat curd cheese	½ cup low-fat curd cheese
1 tablespoon lemon juice	1 tablespoon lemon juice
1 tablespoon olive oil	1 tablespoon olive oil
3 fl oz (90 ml) natural yogurt	⅓ cup plain yogurt
Sea salt and freshly ground black pepper	Sea salt and freshly ground black pepper
1 tablespoon finely chopped chives (optional)	1 tablespoon finely chopped chives (optional)

1. Place the curd cheese in a small bowl and break up with a fork or a small whisk.

2. Gradually beat in the lemon juice, oil and yogurt until thoroughly blended. Add salt, pepper and chives if used. Chill in the refrigerator until required.

SOUR CREAM DRESSING

Imperial (Metric)	American
8 oz (225g) cottage or low-fat curd cheese	1 cup cottage or low-fat curd cheese
¼ pint (150 ml) soured cream	⅔ cup sour cream
Sea salt and freshly ground black pepper	Sea salt and freshly ground black pepper

1. Sieve the cottage cheese (or mash it to a smooth consistency).

2. Blend in the soured cream; adding salt and pepper to taste. Altenatively, whisk together the cottage cheese and soured cream in a blender for 30 seconds. Season.

COTTAGE CHEESE AND CUCUMBER DRESSING

Imperial (Metric)	American
8 oz (225g) cottage cheese	1 cup cottage cheese
¼ cucumber	¼ cucumber
¼ pint (150 ml) natural yogurt	⅔ cup plain yogurt
2 sprigs mint	2 sprigs mint

1. Wipe and roughly chop the cucumber.

2. Combine all the ingredients, place them in a blender and whisk well. Chill in the refrigerator until required.

Variation: Use single (light) cream or 'top of the milk' (half-and-half) in place of the yogurt.

CURD CHEESE DRESSING

Imperial (Metric)	American
4 oz (100g) low-fat curd cheese	½ cup low-fat curd cheese
2 tablespoons lemon juice	2 tablespoons lemon juice
A little single cream or milk	A little light cream or milk
Sea salt and freshly ground black pepper	Sea salt and freshly ground black pepper
1 tablespoon chopped fresh herbs (optional)	1 tablespoon chopped fresh herbs (optional)

1. Place the lemon juice and cheese in a bowl and mash together until smooth and creamy.

2. Pour a little milk into the bowl and continue stirring until the mixture becomes a thick cream, then continue adding milk until it reaches the consistency you require. Add salt, pepper and herbs, if used.

COCONUT DRESSING

Imperial (Metric)	American
8oz (225g) cottage cheese	1 cup cottage cheese
¼ pint (150 ml) single cream or 'top of the milk'	⅔ cup light cream or 'half-and-half'
1 tablespoon clear honey	1 tablespoon clear honey
1oz (25g) desiccated coconut	⅓ cup desiccated coconut

1. Put all the ingredients into a blender and mix together for approximately 30 seconds.

4.
PUDDINGS AND DESSERTS

STRAWBERRY SHORTCAKE

(Serves 8)

Imperial (Metric)	American
4 oz (100g) butter or vegetable margarine	½ cup butter or vegetable margarine
2 oz (50g) raw cane sugar	¼ cup raw cane sugar
5 oz (150g) plain wholemeal flour	1¼ cups plain wholewheat flour
3 oz (75g) hazelnuts, ground and roasted	¾ cup hazelnuts, ground and roasted
6 oz (175g) low-fat curd cheese	¾ cup low-fat curd cheese
1 tablespoon honey	1 tablespoon honey
8 oz (225g) fresh strawberries, hulled and sliced	8 ounces fresh strawberries, hulled and sliced

1. Beat the fat and sugar together until soft. Stir in the flour and ground hazelnuts and mix to a firm dough. Turn onto a floured surface and knead lightly until smooth.

2. Divide in half and roll each piece into an 8 inch (20 cm) round on a baking sheet. For a decorative edge, press the prongs of a fork round the circumference of the rounds. Prick the dough all over with the fork. Mark one round into 8 wedge-shaped portions.

3. Bake both rounds in a preheated oven at 375°F/190°C (Gas Mark 5) for 10 to 15 minutes.

4. Cut through the sections on the marked round while still warm. Transfer both rounds to a wire rack to cool.

5. Beat the curd cheese and honey until smooth, then

carefully spread onto the uncut shortbread round. Cover with the sliced strawberries and arrange the cut triangles on top.

ICED CAROB BROWNIES

(Makes 9)

Imperial (Metric)	American
4 oz (100g) softened butter or vegetable margarine	½ cup softened butter or vegetable margarine
4 oz (100g) raw cane sugar	⅔ cup raw cane sugar
2 eggs, lightly beaten	2 eggs, lightly beaten
2 oz (50g) wholemeal flour	½ cup wholewheat flour
1 oz (25g) carob powder	¼ cup carob powder
2 oz (50g) chopped walnuts	½ cup chopped English walnuts
3 oz (75g) raisins	½ cup raisins
9 walnut halves to decorate	9 English walnut halves to decorate
To make cream icing:	
1 oz (25g) carob powder	*To make cream icing:*
8 oz (225g) low-fat curd cheese	¼ cup carob powder
1-2 tablespoons honey	1 cup low-fat curd cheese
½ teaspoon vanilla essence	1-2 tablespoons honey
½ teaspoon decaffeinated coffee powder	½ teaspoon vanilla extract
	½ teaspoon decaffeinated coffee powder

1. Cream the fat and sugar together until light and fluffy. Gradually add the beaten eggs a little at a time. Add the flour, sift in the carob powder and then stir in the chopped walnuts and raisins.

2. Pour the mixture into a greased and lined 8 inch (20 cm) square cake tin and bake in a preheated oven at 350°F/180°C (Gas Mark 4) for 30-35 minutes until firm to the touch. Remove from the oven and leave to cool on a wire rack.

3. To make the cream icing, sieve the carob powder on to the cheese in a mixing bowl with the rest of the ingredients and beat until smooth.

4. Using a palette knife spread the cream icing evenly over the top, cut into nine squares and place a walnut half on top of each square to decorate.

DEVONSHIRE JUNKET

(Serves 4)

The authentic Devonshire junket is topped with clotted cream. If unobtainable, use lightly whipped double (heavy) cream.

Imperial (Metric)	American
1 pint (570 ml) milk	2½ cups milk
1 tablespoon raw cane sugar	1 tablespoon raw cane sugar
1 teaspoon vegetarian junket rennet	1 teaspoon vegetarian junket rennet
1-2 tablespoons brandy	1-2 tablespoons brandy
¼ pint (150 ml) clotted cream	⅔ cup clotted cream
Ground cinnamon or grated nutmeg	Ground cinnamon or grated nutmeg

1. Put the milk in a saucepan with the sugar and heat to 110°F (45°C). Stir to dissolve the sugar.

2. Remove the pan from the heat, stir in the rennet and brandy, then pour into a china bowl in which you intend to serve the junket. Leave covered in a warm place to set. Do not disturb until the junket is set – any movement will spoil it. (Leave for 1½-2 hours.)

3. Just prior to serving, spread the clotted cream over the surface (if it is stiff, mix with a little fresh cream) and sprinkle with cinnamon or nutmeg.

SIMPLE JUNKET

(Serves 4)

Imperial (Metric)	American
1 pint (570 ml) milk	2½ cups milk
1 tablespoon raw cane sugar	1 tablespoon raw cane sugar
1 teaspoon vegetarian junket rennet	1 teaspoon vegetarian junket rennet
Flavouring (see below)	Flavouring (see below)

1. Put the milk in a saucepan with the sugar and heat to 110°F (45°C). Stir to dissolve the sugar.

2. Pour it into a large china bowl and stir in the rennet, or add the rennet and then divide it between four individual bowls or glasses. Cover and leave in a warm place to set. It takes about 1½-2 hours. When set the junket may be chilled.

FLAVOURINGS FOR THE JUNKET

Nutmeg: Sprinkle a little grated or ground nutmeg over the surface of the junket.

Rum: Add 1-2 tablespoons rum to the milk.

Vanilla, almond, raspberry: Add a few drops of the essence to the milk.

Honey: Substitute 1 tablespoon honey in place of the sugar.

Note: This junket is delicious made with full-cream milk but pasteurized or farm-bottled milk can also be used. However, homogenized, sterilized and UHT milk are not suitable.

PEACH BRÛLÉE

(Serves 4)

Imperial (Metric)	American
5-6 fresh peaches, peeled and sliced	5-6 fresh peaches, peeled and sliced
4 tablespoons orange juice	4 tablespoons orange juice
4 tablespoons reduced sugar peach or apricot jam	4 tablespoons reduced sugar peach or apricot jam
4 oz (100g) low-fat curd cheese	½ cup low-fat curd cheese
¼ pint (150 ml) double or whipping cream	⅔ cup heavy or whipping cream
2 oz (50g) raw cane sugar	⅓ cup raw cane sugar
1 oz (25g) flaked almonds	¼ cup slivered almonds

1. Place the peaches in the base of a shallow ovenproof dish.

2. In a pan, heat the orange juice and jam and pour over the fruit.

3. Mix the cheese and whipped cream together, and spread over the fruit, then sprinkle with the sugar and almonds. Chill in the refrigerator until required.

4. An hour before serving, place under a moderate grill (broiler) for 3-4 minutes until the sugar melts and the nuts turn brown. Then chill again before serving.

Note: To vary the pudding, try substituting the whipped cream with yogurt or soured cream and fruit of your choice.

FRESH FIGS WITH CREAM CHEESE AND RASPBERRY SAUCE

(Serves 4)

Imperial (Metric)	American
1 lb (450g) fresh raspberries, puréed through a nylon sieve	1 pound fresh raspberries, puréed through a nylon sieve
3 tablespoons clear honey	3 tablespoons clear honey
1 teaspoon lemon juice	1 teaspoon lemon juice
12 ripe black figs	12 ripe black figs
12oz (350g) cream cheese	1½ cups cream cheese

1. Place the puréed raspberries into a pan with the honey and place over gentle heat. Taste for sweetness, and add more honey if desired. Simmer for about 10 minutes, stirring, then add the lemon juice, which will enhance the flavour of the raspberries. Set the sauce aside to cool.

2. Using a small, sharp knife, cut the stems from the ripe, fresh figs. Make a small nick at the stem end of each fig, then peel the skin back in strips with the knife. Cut a cross in the top of each peeled fig, slicing down almost to the base of the fruit, then using your thumbs and forefingers lightly press down into the base of each quarter – this will force the fig to open up.

3. Transfer the raspberry sauce into a serving jug. Place three figs on four individual serving plates, then put a dollop of cream cheese in the centre of each fig and pour on the raspberry sauce.

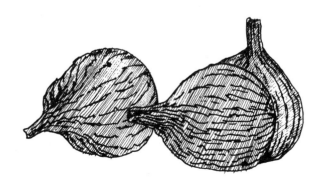

COEUR À LA CRÈME

(Serves 4)

Imperial (Metric)	American
8 oz (225g) low-fat curd cheese	1 cup low-fat curd cheese
¼ pint (150 ml) natural yogurt	⅔ cup plain yogurt
2 tablespoons clear honey	2 tablespoons clear honey
1 egg white	1 egg white
4 6 inch (15 cm) squares of butter muslin	4 6 inch squares of butter muslin
8 oz (225g) fresh strawberries, hulled	8 ounces fresh strawberries, hulled

1. Line four 3 inch (7.5 cm) 'coeur à la crème' porcelain moulds with damp muslin squares, allowing it to hang over the edges.

2. Press the cheese through a fine-meshed nylon sieve into a bowl. Mix in the yogurt and honey. Whisk the egg white until stiff, then fold into the cheese mixture.

3. Spoon the mixture into the moulds and smooth the tops. Place the moulds on a tray and leave them in the refrigerator overnight so that the cheese mixture can set and drain through the holes in the moulds.

4. Invert each of the moulds on to a serving plate. Carefully peel the muslin away from the hearts, which will be marked with the pattern of the draining holes. Serve surrounded with strawberries.

Note: Other fresh soft fruit can be used in place of the strawberries; e.g. raspberries, blackberries, or you can pour a berry purée over the hearts.

RASPBERRY CURD FOOL

(Serves 4-6)

Imperial (Metric)	American
1 lb (450g) raspberries	1 pound raspberries
8 oz (225g) low-fat curd cheese	1 cup low-fat curd cheese
½ pint (300 ml) natural yogurt	1⅓ cups plain yogurt
2-3 tablespoons clear honey	2-3 tablespoons clear honey
2 egg whites	2 egg whites

1. Reserve eight of the best raspberries for decoration and place the remainder in a mixing bowl.

2. Mash the raspberries, then blend in the curd cheese, yogurt and honey to taste. Whisk the egg whites until stiff, then fold into the raspberry mixture.

3. Spoon into four individual serving dishes or one large serving bowl. Decorate with the reserved raspberries and serve immediately.

RUSSIAN-STYLE BLINTZES

(Serves 4)

Imperial (Metric)	American
4oz (100g) wholemeal flour	1 cup wholewheat flour
1 egg	1 egg
½ pint (300 ml) milk	⅓ cup milk
1 tablespoon vegetable oil	1 tablespoon vegetable oil

Filling:

Filling:	
8oz (225g) acid-curd cheese	1 cup acid-curd cheese
1 egg yolk	1 egg yolk
2 tablespoons raw cane sugar	2 tablespoons raw cane sugar
1 teaspoon grated lemon rind	1 teaspoon grated lemon rind
1oz (25g) raisins, washed (optional)	2 tablespoons raisins, washed (optional)
1oz (25g) butter or vegetable margarine	2 tablespoons butter or vegetable margarine
1 tablespoon corn oil	1 tablespoon corn oil
Ground cinnamon	Ground cinnamon
¼ pint (150 ml) soured cream	⅔ cup sour cream

1. Make the pancake (crêpe) batter as instructed on page 95 and cook 8 pancakes (crêpes) on one side only.

2. Rub the curd cheese through a sieve into a bowl. Mix into it the egg yolk, sugar, lemon rind and raisins, if used.

3. Put the filling into the centre of the cooked side of the pancakes (crêpes) and fold over all the edges to make an envelope.

4. Heat the butter or margarine and oil in a large frying-pan. Add the blintzes a few at a time, with the folds underneath. Fry on both sides until crisp and golden brown, turning once. Transfer to a warm serving dish.

5. Repeat with the rest of the pancakes (crêpes) and add to the dish. Sprinkle with cinnamon then top with soured cream. Serve immediately.

STRAWBERRY SUNDAE

(Serves 6)

Imperial (Metric)	American
1¼ lbs fresh ripe strawberries, hulled	1¼ pounds fresh ripe strawberries, hulled
4 oz (100g) cottage or low-fat curd cheese	½ cup cottage or low-fat curd cheese
¼ pint (150 ml) natural yogurt	⅔ cup plain yogurt
2 tablespoons clear honey	2 tablespoons clear honey

1. Divide the strawberries between 6 tall glasses or sundae dishes.

2. Put the cottage cheese, yogurt and honey into a liquidizer and blend until smooth. Alternatively, sieve the cottage cheese, then stir in the yogurt and honey.

3. Pour over the strawberries and chill before serving.

FARMHOUSE ORCHARD SCONES

(Makes 8 scones)

Imperial (Metric)	American
8 oz (225g) wholemeal flour	2 cups wholewheat flour
1 teaspoon baking powder	1 teaspoon baking soda
Pinch of sea salt	Pinch of sea salt
½ teaspoon ground cinnamon	½ teaspoon ground cinnamon
2 oz (50g) butter or vegetable margarine	¼ cup butter or vegetable margarine
1 beaten egg with enough milk added to make ¼ pint (150 ml) liquid	1 beaten egg with enough milk added to make ⅔ cup liquid
Milk for brushing	Milk for brushing
Cracked wheat (optional)	Cracked wheat (optional)
12 oz (350g) eating apples	12 ounces eating apples
4 oz (100g) low-fat curd cheese	½ cup low-fat curd cheese

1. Sift the flour, baking powder, salt and ground cinnamon together into a large mixing bowl, and add the bran from the sieve. Rub in the fat until the mixture resembles fine breadcrumbs. Add the egg and milk and mix to a soft dough.

2. Turn out onto a floured surface and knead very lightly until smooth. Mould into a 7 inch (18 cm) round and place on a lightly oiled baking tray. Mark into eight wedges with a sharp knife and brush with milk. Sprinkle the top with cracked wheat, if liked.

3. Bake in a preheated hot oven 425°F/220°C (Gas Mark 7), for 15-20 minutes, until well risen and firm to the touch. Slide out onto a wire rack to cool slightly.

4. Meanwhile, wash, core and slice the apples and put them into a saucepan. Add 1 tablespoon of water and cook over gentle heat until soft; about 15 minutes. Remove from the heat, sieve and allow to cool before stirring into the cheese.

5. Break the scones apart while still warm, split each wedge and sandwich together with the cheese and apple mixture. Best eaten on the day of making.

CREAM CHEESE ICING (FROSTING) OR FILLING

Imperial (Metric)	American
8oz (225g) cream cheese	1 cup cream cheese
2 tablespoons honey	2 tablespoons honey
1-2 teaspoons vanilla essence	1-2 teaspoons vanilla extract

1. Place the cream cheese in a bowl and beat with a wooden spoon to soften. Blend in the honey and 1-2 teaspoons of vanilla essence (extract). Use as a filling or icing (frosting) for sponges and small cakes.

Variations: Add a little finely grated orange or lemon rind; a pinch of ground cinnamon or spice; or a little drop of your favourite liqueur.

CREAM CHEESE SCONES

(Makes 8 scones)

Imperial (Metric)	American
4oz (100g) butter or vegetable margarine	½ cup butter or vegetable margarine
8oz (225g) 81% wholemeal self-raising flour	2 cups 81% wholewheat self-raising flour
Pinch of sea salt	Pinch of sea salt
4oz (100g) cream cheese	½ cup cream cheese

1. Rub the fat into the flour and salt until it resembles breadcrumbs. Mix in the cream cheese and bind the mixture together until the dough forms.

2. Roll out on a floured board to a thickness of ¾ inch (2 cm). Cut into 2 inch (5 cm) round with a fluted cutter and place on a lightly oiled baking tray.

3. Bake in a preheated hot oven 425°F/220°C (Gas Mark 7) for 15 minutes or until firm to the touch.

RICOTTA-STUFFED PEACHES

(Serves 6)

Imperial (Metric)	American
6 large firm, peaches	6 large firm, peaches
6oz (175g) fresh Ricotta or low-fat curd cheese	¾ cup fresh Ricotta or low-fat curd cheese
1 egg	1 egg
2 tablespoons honey	2 tablespoons honey
1oz (25g) mixed candied peel	2 tablespoons mixed candied peel
A few drops of almond essence	A few drops of almond extract
Flaked almonds to decorate (optional)	Slivered almonds to decorate (optional)

1. Plunge the peaches into boiling water for 2 to 3 minutes, then peel off the skin. Slit the peaches round the natural crease and remove the stones.

2. Mix together the cheese, egg and honey, then stir in the candied peel and almond essence. Divide this mixture evenly between the peach halves. Top with the flaked almonds if liked, and arrange in a buttered, shallow ovenproof dish.

3. Bake in a preheated oven at 350°F/180°C (Gas Mark 4) for 25 to 30 minutes until the peaches are tender. Serve hot.

PLUM AND CURD CHEESE SLICE

Imperial (Metric)	American
For the base:	*For the base:*
8 oz (225 g) self-raising wholemeal flour	2 cups self-raising wholewheat flour
¼ level teaspoon sea salt	¼ level teaspoon sea salt
4 oz (100 g) butter or vegetable margarine	½ cup butter or vegetable margarine
2 oz (50 g) raw cane sugar	⅓ cup raw cane sugar
1 egg, beaten	1 egg, beaten
For the filling:	*For the filling:*
1 lb (450 g) red plums	1 pound red plums
4 oz (100 g) low-fat curd cheese	½ cup low-fat curd cheese
2 oz (50 g) raw cane sugar	⅓ cup raw cane sugar
½ oz (15 g) butter or vegetable margarine	1 tablespoon butter or vegetable margarine

1. Place the flour and salt in a mixing bowl. Rub in the butter or margarine until it resembles fine breadcrumbs. Stir in the sugar, then bind together with the egg to form a stiff dough.

2. Grease a 8 x 12 inch (20 x 30 cm) Swiss roll tin and line with greaseproof paper. Roll out the dough to fit the tin.

3. Cut plums in half. Remove stones and roughly chop.

4. Cover pastry with the chopped plums and spread the curd cheese over the top. Sprinkle with a layer of sugar, and dot with the butter or margarine.

5. Bake in a preheated moderately hot oven, 375°F/190°C (Gas Mark 5) for 35-40 minutes. Cool and cut into squares.

BANANA AND COTTAGE CHEESE MILK SHAKE

(Serves 4)

Imperial (Metric)	American
½ pint (300 ml) cold milk	1⅓ cups cold milk
4 medium-sized ripe bananas, mashed	4 medium-sized ripe bananas, mashed
4 oz (100g) cottage cheese	½ cup cottage cheese
1 tablespoon clear honey	1 tablespoon clear honey
5 ice cubes	5 ice cubes

1. Place all the ingredients in a blender or food processor and process until smooth and frothy. (If you would like the shake still thinner, add more cold milk.) Serve immediately.

STRAWBERRY CHEESE MOUSSE

(Serves 4-6)

Imperial (Metric)	American
12 oz (350g) medium-fat curd cheese	1½ cups medium-fat curd cheese
2 oz (50g) raw cane sugar	⅓ cup raw cane sugar
12 oz (350g) fresh strawberries, hulled	¾ pound fresh strawberries, hulled
¼ pint (150 ml) double cream	⅔ cup heavy cream
2 egg whites	2 egg whites

1. Beat the cheese and sugar together until soft, smooth and creamy.

2. Reserve 4 strawberries for decoration and set aside. Purée the rest of the strawberries in a liquidizer or push through a sieve. Stir the purée into the cheese mixture.

3. Whip the cream until it just holds its shape, then fold into the mixture.

4. Whisk the egg whites until stiff and standing in peaks and fold in.

5. Chill and serve decorated with the reserved strawberries and extra whipped cream, if liked.

DATE AND COTTAGE CHEESE ICE CREAM

(Serves 4-6)

Imperial (Metric)	American
8oz (225g) fresh dates	8 ounces fresh dates
1lb (450g) cottage cheese	2 cups cottage cheese
4oz (100g) set honey	⅓ cup set honey
1 teaspoon vanilla essence	1 teaspoon vanilla extract
4 tablespoons double cream, whipped	¼ cup heavy cream, whipped
2 tablespoons sweet sherry or Marsala	2 tablespoons sweet sherry or Marsala
2 egg whites	2 egg whites
1oz (25g) hazelnuts, coarsely chopped	¼ cup hazelnuts, coarsely chopped
3 tablespoons clear honey	3 tablespoons clear honey
1 tablespoon fresh orange juice	1 tablespoon fresh orange juice

1. Cut the dates in half and remove the stones. Reserve half the dates and chop the remainder.

2. Sieve the cottage cheese into a bowl. Warm the honey gently in a saucepan until it is runny. Beat this into the cheese. Add the vanilla essence. Fold in the whipped cream and sherry or Marsala.

3. Whisk the egg whites until stiff and fold into the mixture with the chopped dates. Pour into a 1½ pounds (675g) loaf tin. Cover and freeze.

4. When frozen, turn out and cut into slices. Mix the remaining dates, hazelnuts, honey and orange juice together. Place the ice cream in individual serving dishes and spoon the date mixture over the top. Serve immediately.

COTTAGE CHEESE PANCAKES (CRÊPES)

(Makes 10-12)

Imperial (Metric)	American
8oz (225g) cottage cheese	1 cup cottage cheese
1oz (25g) 81% wholemeal flour	¼ cup 81% wholewheat flour
3 eggs, well beaten	3 eggs, well beaten
2 tablespoons milk	2 tablespoons milk
1 tablespoon vegetable oil	1 tablespoon vegetable oil
Pinch of sea salt (optional)	Pinch of sea salt (optional)

1. Sieve the cottage cheese into a mixing bowl. Stir in the flour and salt if using, then add the eggs, milk and oil, beating in well.

2. Heat a lightly oiled griddle or heavy frying pan (skillet). Pour in enough batter to make a 5 inch (12.5 cm) thin pancake (crêpe), and fry until golden brown on both sides, turning once. Repeat with the remaining batter, making sure that the pan or griddle is well greased before making each pancake.

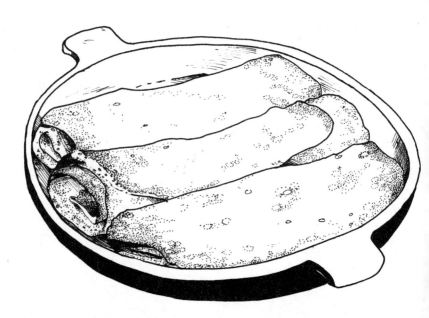

NECTARINE AND RASPBERRY FILLED PANCAKES (CRÊPES)

(Serves 4)

Imperial (Metric)	American
Pancake batter:	*Crêpe batter:*
4 oz (100g) wholemeal flour	1 cup wholewheat flour
Pinch of sea salt (optional)	Pinch of sea salt (optional)
1 egg	1 egg
½ pint (300 ml) skimmed milk or use half milk and half water	1⅓ cups skimmed milk or use half milk and half water
1 tablespoon oil	1 tablespoon oil
Vegetable oil for frying	Vegetable oil for frying
Filling:	*Filling:*
8 oz (225g) low-fat curd cheese	1 cup low-fat curd cheese
3 tablespoons natural yogurt	3 tablespoons plain yogurt
1-2 tablespoons clear honey	1-2 tablespoons clear honey
2 nectarines, sliced and dipped in lemon juice	2 nectarines, sliced and dipped in lemon juice
6 oz (175g) fresh raspberries	6 ounces fresh raspberries

1. Sift the flour into a mixing bowl with the salt, if using. Make a well in the centre, add the egg, then gradually stir in half the milk and oil. Beat thoroughly until smooth. Add the remaining milk. Leave to stand for at least 30 minutes.

2. Lightly oil a 7 inch (18 cm) non-stick frying pan (skillet) and place over a moderate heat. Pour in enough batter to cover the base. Cook until the underside is lightly browned, then turn and cook the other side. Repeat with the remaining batter to make 8 pancakes (crêpes).

3. For the filling, beat together the curd cheese, yogurt and honey until light.

4. To fill the pancakes (crêpes), place on a flat surface and spread thinly with the cheese mixture. Fold the pancakes (crêpes) into four, making a cornet shape. Slip a few raspberries and a slice or two of the nectarines in the top layer of the cornet. Serve immediately.

COTTAGE CHEESE AND DATE TEABREAD

(Makes one 1 lb/450g loaf)

Imperial (Metric)	American
8oz (225g) self-raising wholemeal flour	2 cups self-raising wholewheat flour
½ teaspoon mixed spice	½ teaspoon mixed spice
1oz (25g) raw cane sugar	2 tablespoons raw cane sugar
2oz (50g) butter or polyunsaturated margarine	¼ cup butter or polyunsaturated margarine
2 eggs	2 eggs
4oz (100g) cottage cheese	½ cup cottage cheese
3 tablespoons milk	3 tablespoons milk
Juice and grated rind of 1 medium orange	Juice and grated rind of 1 medium orange
1oz (25g) walnuts, chopped	¼ cup English walnuts, chopped
2oz (50g) dates, chopped	⅓ cup dates, chopped

1. Sift the flour and mixed spice into a mixing bowl, adding the bran left in the sieve. Stir in the sugar and rub in the butter or margarine until the mixture resembles breadcrumbs.

2. In a separate bowl, beat the eggs with the cottage cheese, milk, and one tablespoon of juice from the orange, then add to the dry ingredients with the walnuts, dates and grated orange rind. Mix well.

3. Spoon the mixture into a greased 1 pound (450g) loaf tin and smooth the top. Bake the teabread in the centre of a preheated moderate oven, 350°F/180°C (Gas Mark 4) for 45 minutes, or until well risen and golden brown. Leave in the tin for 10 minutes, then turn onto a wire rack to cool.

MAIDS OF HONOUR

(Makes about 18)

Tradition has it that these little English tartlets took their name from the Maids of Honour who attended Elizabeth I at Richmond Palace.

Imperial (Metric)	American
8 oz (225g) packet frozen wholemeal puff pastry	8 ounce packet frozen wholewheat puff pastry
2 oz (50g) unsalted butter	¼ cup unsalted butter
4 oz (100g) fresh curds	½ cup fresh curds
2 eggs	2 eggs
1 tablespoon brandy	1 tablespoon brandy
2 oz (50g) ground almonds	½ cup ground almonds
1 tablespoon light raw cane sugar	1 tablespoon light raw cane sugar
A few currants (optional)	A few currants (optional)

1. Grease the insides of 18 x 2¼ inch (6 cm) bun tins 1¼ inches (3 cm) deep. Roll out the pastry on a lightly-floured board and use to line the tins. Chill while making the filling.

2. Place the butter in a bowl and beat with a wooden spoon until creamy. Rub the curds through a sieve into the bowl.

3. Whisk the eggs and brandy together and add to the curds, with the ground almonds and sugar.

4. Spoon the mixture into the chilled pastry cases to half-full, (more than this will overflow during cooking) and if liked sprinkle currants over the top.

5. Bake in the centre of a preheated oven, 425°F/220°C (Gas Mark 7) for 15-20 minutes, until well risen and golden-brown. Serve really fresh.

5.
CHEESECAKES

ST. CLEMENT'S PANCAKE (CRÊPE) GÂTEAU

(Serves 4-6)

So called because of the children's nursery rhyme imitating London church bells, '"Oranges and Lemons," say the Bells of St. Clement's'.

Imperial (Metric)	American
8-10 medium-sized pancakes made from ½ pint (300 ml) basic batter (see page 95) with a few drops of real almond essence added	8-10 medium-sized crêpes made from 1⅓ cups basic batter (see page 95) with a few drops of real almond extract added
2 large oranges	2 large oranges
8oz (225g) cottage cheese	1 cup cottage cheese
8oz (225g) low-fat curd cheese	1 cup low-fat curd cheese
2oz (50g) flaked almonds	½ cup slivered almonds
½ teaspoon real vanilla essence	½ teaspoon real vanilla extract
2oz (50g) clear honey	2 tablespoons clear honey
Juice of 1 lemon	Juice of 1 lemon
1oz (25g) flaked almonds (toasted)	¼ cup slivered almonds (toasted)

1. Stack the pancakes (crêpes) on a heatproof plate, with a piece of greaseproof paper between each one. Place over a pan of simmering water to keep hot while making the filling.

2. Slice the top and bottom off the oranges, then using a serrated knife and a sawing motion, cut away the peel, pith and outer membrane. Slice the oranges and set aside.

3. Press the cottage cheese through a sieve. Mix with the curd cheese, almonds and vanilla essence.

4. In a small pan, warm the honey and lemon juice together. Brush a pancake (crêpe) with this mixture, then spread a little of the cheese and almond mixture over it. Repeat for four more pancakes (crêpes), stacking them one on top of the other on a heatproof dish.

5. Lay half of the orange slices over the top of the cheese mixture. Continue layering with the remaining pancakes (crêpes) and filling, finishing with a pancake (crêpe). Reserve a little of the honey and lemon mixture for decoration.

6. Cover with foil and bake in a preheated moderate oven, 350°F/180°C (Gas Mark 4) for 15 minutes or until heated through.

7. Just before serving, brush the top with the reserved honey and lemon mixture. Arrange the remaining orange slices and the toasted almonds on top of the gâteau. Serve immediately, cutting it in wedges like a pie.

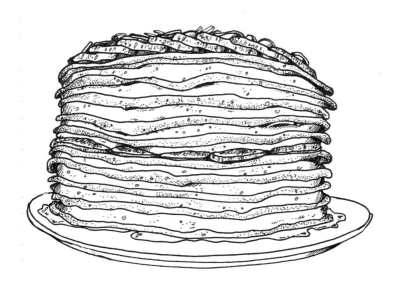

OVERNIGHT CHEESECAKE

(Serves 6-8)

Imperial (Metric)	American
For the base:	*For the base:*
2 oz (50g) butter or vegetable margarine	¼ cup butter or vegetable margarine
1 tablespoon raw cane sugar	1 tablespoon raw cane sugar
2 oz (50g) chopped walnuts	½ cup chopped English walnuts
6 oz (175g) digestive wholemeal biscuits, crushed	6 ounces Graham crackers, crushed
For the filling:	*For the filling:*
1 lb (450g) medium-fat curd cheese	2 cups medium-fat curd cheese
2 eggs, beaten	2 eggs, beaten
4 oz (100g) raw cane sugar	⅔ cup raw cane sugar
1 tablespoon lemon juice	1 tablespoon lemon juice
½ teaspoon real vanilla essence	½ teaspoon real vanilla extract
For the topping:	*For the topping:*
½ pint (300 ml) soured cream	1⅓ cups soured cream
2 tablespoons clear honey	2 tablespoons clear honey
½ teaspoon real vanilla essence	½ teaspoon real vanilla extract

1. Melt the butter or margarine in a pan. Remove from the heat and stir in the sugar, walnuts and biscuit crumbs. Mix well and press into the base of a lightly oiled 8½ inch (21.5 cm) springform loose-bottomed cake tin. Chill while making the filling.

2. Make the filling by beating the curd cheese, eggs and sugar together until they are smooth and creamy. Add the lemon juice and vanilla essence and mix thoroughly. Spoon over the biscuit base and bake in a preheated moderately hot oven, 375°F/190°C (Gas Mark 5) for 25-30 minutes or until set. While baking, mix together the soured cream, honey and vanilla essence for the topping.

3. Remove the cheesecake from the oven and turn up the temperature to 425°F/220°C (Gas Mark 7). Pour the soured cream mixture on to the cheesecake over the

back of a spoon so that it spreads gently and evenly all over the top; return to the oven and bake for 10 minutes. Remove, and cool in the tin. Cover with foil and refrigerate for at least 12 hours before serving.

Note: Although the soured cream layer will not be set when removed from the oven, it will firm as the cheesecake cools. Chilling overnight improves the flavour and texture of the cheesecake and makes it easier to cut.

ALMOND CHEESECAKE

(Serves 6-8)

Imperial (Metric)	American
For the base:	*For the base:*
2 oz (50g) butter or vegetable margarine, melted	¼ cup butter or vegetable margarine, melted
4 oz (100g) digestive wholemeal biscuits, crushed	4 ounces Graham crackers, crushed
For the filling:	*For the filling:*
8 oz (225g) cottage cheese	1 cup cottage cheese
8 oz (225g) medium-fat curd cheese	1 cup medium-fat curd cheese
1 oz (25g) raw cane sugar	2 tablespoons raw cane sugar
3 eggs, separated	3 eggs, separated
2 oz (50g) ground almonds	½ cup ground almonds
2 oz (50g) chopped mixed peel	⅓ cup chopped mixed peel
1 tablespoon wholemeal semolina	1 tablespoon wholewheat semolina
1 tablespoon brandy	1 tablespoon brandy
½ teaspoon real almond essence	½ teaspoon real almond extract
For decoration:	*For decoration:*
Toasted almonds	Toasted almonds

1. Combine the biscuit crumbs and melted fat thoroughly, using a wooden spoon. Press into the base of a lightly oiled 8½ inch (21.5 cm) springform, loose-bottomed cake tin. Chill while making the filling.

2. Sieve the cottage cheese into a bowl and mix with the curd cheese. Beat in the sugar and egg yolks until creamy. Add the ground almonds, mixed peel, semolina, brandy and almond essence and mix in thoroughly. Whisk the egg whites until stiff and gently fold into the cheese mixture.

3. Pour this mixture over the biscuit base and gently smooth over the top. Bake in the centre of a preheated oven, 325°F/170°C (Gas Mark 3) for 1-1¼ hours or until just firm to the touch. Cover loosely with greaseproof paper if it begins to over-brown while baking.

4. Turn off the oven and leave the cheesecake to cool gradually in the oven. When cool, remove from the oven, and when cold run a knife round the sides between the cake and tin. Place tin evenly on a jar, coffee tin etc., release spring clip and remove tin sides carefully.

5. Turn the cheesecake out onto its serving plate and decorate with the toasted almonds by pressing them into the surface of the cheesecake in a ring around the edge.

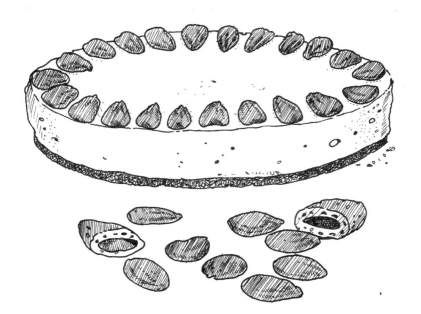

PASKHA (Russian Cheesecake)

(Serves 8-10)

'*Paskha*' means Easter in Russian and it is also the name given to a traditional Easter dessert. In Russian families, this is often made in a special wooden mould with the letters XB – standing for 'Christ is Risen'. The shape of your *paskha* will depend on what container you have which has a drainage hole or holes. The traditional mould has a small opening at the narrow end to drain off any moisture; a new terracotta flower pot can be used to produce an authentic shape or pierce holes in cottage cheese cartons.

If using a flower pot, soak it for 1 hour in cold water to rid it of any flavour of raw clay which could taint the dessert. When dry, bake in an oven at 250°F/130°C (Gas Mark ½) for 30 minutes. Cool.

Imperial (Metric)	American
1½lbs (680g) curd cheese	2½ cups curd cheese
2oz (50g) butter or soft vegetable margarine	¼ cup butter or soft vegetable margarine
1 large egg, beaten	1 large egg, beaten
1oz (25g) set honey	1 tablespoon set honey
2oz (50g) chopped blanched almonds	½ cup chopped blanched almonds
2oz (50g) chopped mixed candied peel	⅓ cup chopped mixed candied peel
2oz (50g) raisins	⅓ cup raisins
2oz (50g) currants	⅓ cup currants
¼ teaspoon real vanilla essence	¼ teaspoon real vanilla extract
Grated lemon rind (optional)	Grated lemon rind (optional)

1. Press the well-drained curd cheese through a sieve into a bowl. Beat the softened butter into a quarter of the curd cheese until light, then add all the remaining ingredients and mix very thoroughly.

2. Line the flower pot or container used as a mould with sterilized muslin (cheesecloth). Leave enough material to fold over the top of the container.

3. Fill with the cheese mixture pressing it firmly into the pot. Fold the loose ends of the muslin (cheesecloth)

lining over the top of the filling so that the mixture is completely covered.

4. Put a plate or saucer – slightly smaller than the mould – on top of the wrapped cheese mixture. Place a weight on top – use a 2 lb (1 kilo) weight for a large pot of cheese, a 6 oz (175g) for a carton. Place the pot or cartons on a rack with a tray underneath to catch the liquid, and refrigerate the dessert overnight or for 24 hours.

5. When ready to serve, unmould and carefully remove the cloth which will leave a neat 'weave' pattern on the surface. Decorate the *paskha* with almonds, raisins and candied peel, if desired.

Note: For this recipe it is important that the cheese is very smooth and as 'dry' as possible. The best cheese to use is low or medium fat curd cheese. If you want to use cottage cheese, rub it through a sieve.

CAROB CHEESECAKE

(Serves 4-6)

Imperial (Metric)	American
For the flan case:	*For the flan case:*
3 oz (75g) butter or vegetable margarine	⅓ cup butter or vegetable margarine
1 oz (25g) honey	1 tablespoon honey
3 oz (75g) porridge oats	¾ cup rolled oats
3 oz (75g) muesli	½ cup muesli
2 tablespoons sunflower seeds	2 tablespoons sunflower seeds
For the filling:	*For the filling:*
1 lb (450g) cottage cheese	2 cups cottage cheese
1 tablespoon carob powder	1 tablespoon carob powder
2 teaspoons dissolved decaffeinated coffee granules	2 teaspoons dissolved decaffeinated coffee granules
6 fl oz (178 ml) single cream	⅔ cup light cream
2 oz (50g) honey	2 tablespoons honey
Pinch of ground cinnamon	Pinch of ground cinnamon
Grated carob and whipped cream to decorate	Grated carob and whipped cream to decorate

1. Melt the butter and honey together into a pan. Remove from the heat and mix in the rest of the flan case ingredients. Press into the base and sides of a lightly oiled 8 inch (20 cm) flan dish. Chill in the refrigerator to harden.

2. To make the filling, place all the filling ingredients into a food processor or liquidizer and blend until smooth. Spread evenly into the chilled flan case and place in the refrigerator until firm – about 1 hour. Before serving, decorate with grated carob and rosettes of whipped cream.

Note: This cheesecake is best eaten on the same day, before the flan case becomes soft.

ORANGE GÂTEAU

(Serves 8)

Imperial (Metric)	American
6oz (175g) butter or vegetable margarine	¾ cup butter or vegetable margarine
4oz (100g) light Muscovado sugar	⅔ cup light Muscovado sugar
3 eggs, well beaten	3 eggs, well beaten
6oz (175g) wholemeal self-raising flour	1½ cups wholewheat self-raising flour
Grated rind and juice of 1 small orange	Grated rind and juice of 1 small orange

Filling and topping:	*Filling and topping:*
12oz (350g) medium-fat curd cheese	1½ cups medium-fat curd cheese
2 tablespoons honey	2 tablespoons honey
¼ pint (150ml) thick-set natural yogurt	⅔ cup thick-set plain yogurt
1 large orange	1 large orange
4oz (100g) chopped walnuts	¾ cup chopped English walnuts

1. Grease and line the base of two 8 inch (20 cm) sandwich tins.

2. In a large bowl cream together the fat and sugar until light and fluffy, then gradually add the eggs, beating well after each addition. Fold in the flour with a metal spoon or spatula. Stir in the rind and orange juice.

3. Divide the mixture between the prepared tins and level the surfaces. Place in the centre of a preheated oven at 350°F/180°C (Gas Mark 4) for 25 to 30 minutes until the cakes are well risen and spring back when lightly pressed. Leave in the tins for a few minutes then turn out and cool on a wire rack.

4. Beat together the curd cheese, honey and yogurt until smooth. Spread half of the mixture on one of the cakes. Peel and cut away the pith from the orange. Cut between each segment to release the flesh. Reserving a few segments for decoration, chop the remainder and arrange on top of the filling. Place the other cake on top: spread the rest of the cheese mixture over the top and sides of the cake. Press the chopped walnuts onto the sides. Decorate with the reserved orange segments.

CAROB CHERRY ROLL

(Serves 4-6)

Imperial (Metric)	American
3 eggs	3 eggs
3 oz (75g) clear honey	¼ cup clear honey
1 tablespoon hot water	1 tablespoon hot water
2 oz (50g) plain wholemeal flour	½ cup plain wholewheat flour
1 oz (25g) carob powder	¼ cup carob powder
Filling:	*Filling:*
8 oz (225g) red cherries	8 ounces red cherries
8 oz (225g) low-fat curd cheese	1 cup low-fat curd cheese
2-3 tablespoons milk	2-3 tablespoons milk
1 tablespoon honey	1 tablespoon honey
Carob bar to decorate	Carob bar to decorate

1. Line a 9 x 12 inch (23 x 30 cm) Swiss roll tin with greaseproof paper or non-stick vegetable parchment paper, making sure that the edges protrude about ½ inch (12 mm) above sides of tin on all sides. Brush with oil (this is not necessary with non-stick parchment paper).

2. Place the eggs and honey in a bowl and whisk with an electric whisk, or place the bowl over a pan of simmering water and whisk with a hand whisk until light and foamy and the whisk, when lifted, leaves a thick trail or ribbon on the surface. (It is very much easier if you use an electric whisk.)

3. Sift the flour with the carob powder, then sieve again on to the egg mixture. Tip in the remaining bran, and fold all together carefully with a metal spoon. Add hot water and mix in lightly.

4. Pour the mixture into the prepared tin and level the surface by gently tilting the tin. Bake in a preheated oven at 425°F/220°C (Gas Mark 7) for 10-12 minutes until cooked and springy to the touch.

5. Turn out Swiss roll on to a large piece of greaseproof paper or non-stick vegetable parchment. Peel off the baking paper. (To help make the sponge pliable, you can place the paper over a tea towel lightly wrung out in

hot water.) Trim the edges with a sharp knife and make a dent along one short end, about ½ inch (12 mm) from the edge. Roll up with a clean sheet of paper inside and leave to cool on a wire rack.

6. To make filling: wash, dry and stone the cherries, reserving a few whole ones for decoration and roughly chop the remainder. Beat the cheese with the milk and honey until the mixture is smooth. Stir in the chopped cherries into about two-thirds of the cheese mixture.

7. Unroll the Swiss roll, remove paper and spread the cherry and cheese mixture over, almost to the edges. Roll up carefully.

8. Place the remaining cheese mixture in a piping bag with a large star nozzle and pipe on the top of the roll. Decorate with the reserved cherries and grated carob.

YORKSHIRE CURD TART

(Serves 6)

A traditional recipe.

Imperial (Metric)	American
6oz (175g) wholemeal shortcrust pastry (page 40)	6 ounces wholewheat shortcrust pastry (page 40)
8oz (225g) acid curd cheese	1 cup acid curd cheese
1½oz (40g) melted butter	3 tablespoons melted butter
1½oz (40g) raw cane sugar	3 tablespoons raw cane sugar
1 large egg, beaten	1 large egg, beaten
Grated rind of ½ lemon	Grated rind of ½ lemon
½ teaspoon ground nutmeg	½ teaspoon ground nutmeg
1oz (25g) currants	¼ cup currants

1. Roll out the pastry and use to line a 7 inch (18 cm) flan ring placed on a greased baking sheet.

2. Beat the curd cheese with the butter, sugar, egg, lemon rind and nutmeg. Stir in the currants. Turn the mixture into the pastry case.

3. Bake in a preheated moderately hot oven 375°F/190°C (Gas Mark 5) for 35 to 40 minutes. Serve just warm or cold.

BAKED CURD CHEESECAKE

(Serves 4-6)

Imperial (Metric)	American
Pastry:	*Pastry:*
4 oz (100g) wholemeal flour	1 cup wholewheat flour
2 oz (50g) butter or vegetable margarine	¼ cup butter or vegetable margarine
1 egg yolk	1 egg yolk
Cold water to mix	Cold water to mix
Filling:	*Filling:*
3 tablespoons raw sugar apricot jam	3 tablespoons raw sugar apricot jam
2 eggs, separated	2 eggs, separated
8 oz (225g) fresh curds	1 cup fresh curds
2 oz (50g) sultanas	⅓ cup golden seedless raisins
Finely grated rind and juice of 1 lemon	Finely grated rind and juice of 1 lemon

1. Sift the flour into a bowl and add the bran from the sieve. Rub in the butter or margarine until the mixture resembles fine breadcrumbs. Add the egg yolk and just enough cold water to mix to a firm dough. Roll out and use to line a 7 to 8 inch (18 to 20 cm) flan tin or ring placed on a baking sheet. Spread the base with jam.

2. Put the sugar and egg yolks in a bowl, then beat together until light. Add the cheese, sultanas, lemon rind and juice. Beat well until thoroughly mixed. Whisk the egg whites until stiff and standing in peaks, then fold into the cheese mixture.

3. Spread mixture over jam. Smooth top and bake in the centre of a preheated moderate oven 350°F/180°C (Gas Mark 4) for about 40-45 minutes, or until it is set and the top is golden brown. Cool before serving.

CONTINENTAL CHEESECAKE

(Serves 8)

Imperial (Metric)	American
For the base:	*For the base:*
6oz (175g) wholemeal digestive biscuits	6 ounces Graham crackers
2oz (50g) butter or polyunsaturated margarine	¼ cup butter or polyunsaturated margarine
For the filling:	*For the filling:*
4oz (100g) butter or polyunsaturated margarine	½ cup butter or polyunsaturated margarine
4oz (100g) light raw cane sugar	⅔ cup light raw cane sugar
3 eggs	3 eggs
2oz (50g) self-raising wholemeal flour, sieved	½ cup self-raising wholewheat flour, sieved
1lb (450g) medium-fat curd cheese	1 pound medium-fat curd cheese
1 teaspoon real vanilla essence	1 teaspoon real vanilla extract
Grated rind and juice of ½ lemon	Grated rind and juice of ½ lemon
3oz (75g) sultanas	½ cup golden seedless raisins
For the topping:	*For the topping:*
¼ pint (150 ml) soured cream	⅔ cup soured cream
1 tablespoon clear honey	1 tablespoon clear honey
Nutmeg	Nutmeg

1. Put the biscuits into a polythene bag and crush them with a rolling pin. (The biscuits may be crushed in a liquidizer.)

2. Melt the butter or margarine in a saucepan over a low heat. Add the crushed biscuits and stir until they are well mixed. Press into the base of an 8½ inch (21.5 cm) springform, loose-bottomed cake tin.

3. Cream the butter or margarine and sugar together until light and fluffy. Beat in the eggs one at a time, adding a little of the flour if the mixture starts to curdle.

4. In a separate bowl, work the cheese with a fork or beat

with a wooden spoon to smooth out any lumps. Stir in the vanilla essence, lemon rind and juice, then add to the creamed mixture. Fold in the remaining flour and lastly the sultanas.

5. Spoon the mixture over the biscuit base and level the surface. Bake in the centre of a preheated oven, 325°F/170°C (Gas Mark 3) for about 1¼ hours until just firm to the touch – reduce to 300°F/150°C (Gas Mark 2) if the top of the cheesecake starts to overbrown. Cool in the turned-off oven. When cold, run a sharp knife round the inside of the tin to loosen the cheesecake, then remove the sides of the tin.

6. To make the topping, turn the soured cream into a bowl and stir in the honey. Spread the sweetened cream over the top of the cheesecake and finely grate a little nutmeg over the cream.

CHEESECAKE SPONGE FLAN

(Serves 4-6)

Imperial (Metric)	American
Flan case:	*Flan case:*
2 oz (50g) butter or vegetable margarine	¼ cup butter or vegetable margarine
2 oz (50g) clear honey	2 tablespoons clear honey
2 eggs	2 eggs
3 oz (75g) wholemeal flour, sieved	¾ cup wholewheat flour, sieved
Filling:	*Filling:*
8 oz (225g) low-fat curd cheese	1 cup low-fat curd cheese
1 oz (25g) raw cane sugar	2 tablespoons raw cane sugar
3 fl oz (85 ml) double cream	6 tablespoons thick cream
1 egg, separated	1 egg, separated
1 tablespoon dark rum	1 tablespoon dark rum
1 oz (25g) raisins	2 tablespoons raisins

1. Grease a 7 inch (18 cm) sponge flan tin.

2. Cream the butter or margarine and honey together until light and fluffy. Gradually add the beaten eggs, adding some flour if the mixture starts to curdle. Fold in the flour and spoon the mixture into the prepared tin.

3. Bake in a preheated oven, 350°F/180°C (Gas Mark 4) for 20 to 25 minutes, or until firm to the touch. Turn out and cool on a wire rack.

4. Cream together all the filling ingredients except the egg white. Whisk the egg white until fairly stiff and add to the blended mixture. Fold in carefully. Spoon into the flan case and smooth top. Chill, if liked.

Note: It is advisable to eat this cheesecake within 24 hours of making.

PART TWO: HOME-MADE CHEESES

6.
AN INTRODUCTION TO CHEESEMAKING

Cheesemaking is based on the principle that certain enzymes and acids can cause the milk to coagulate, or clot, forming solid curds and liquid whey. Raw milk will do this naturally if it is left to sour. This is because the lactic acid bacteria in the milk feed on the milk sugar (lactose) to produce lactic acid. The longer it is left the more acid it becomes, until it finally curdles. The separation is caused by the effect that the acid has upon the protein 'casein' in the milk. This natural process can be hastened by subjecting the milk to gentle warmth. Obversely, strong heat has the opposite effect. Raw milk containing such bacteria is not generally sold in shops: pasteurized milk, which is universally available, has been heat-treated to kill all the disease-causing organisms and ensures that the milk is absolutely safe to drink. Unfortunately this also destroys most, but not all, of the lactic acid-producing bacteria that cause the milk to sour or ripen. Whilst this does of course improve the keeping qualities of the milk, it does mean that cheese made from pasteurized milk will not be able to develop such a good flavour.

In order to make cheese from pasteurized milk, you must first reintroduce the appropriate bacteria into the milk. This is known as adding a *starter* – a special culture of lactic acid-producing bacteria – to sour and curdle the milk. It is possible to buy commercial starters from certain laboratories in a freeze-dried sachet, but these are expensive and make cheesemaking rather complicated. The best alternative is to use commercially cultured buttermilk, a by-product of butter-making that is thickened by bacterial action. This is widely available, cheap and gives excellent results. (If a small amount of buttermilk is added to warm milk, the bacteria will multiply rapidly and within a day or less will produce enough acid to curdle the milk.) The bacteria are almost identical to those used in cheese starters. It is also possible to make your own specialized starter from a piece of shop-bought cheese. The procedure is explained in due course in this book. Another way to curdle the milk is to use lemon juice, vinegar or an acid such as cream of tartar.

Soured milk, whether it is unpasteurized (raw milk) that has been left to sour naturally or pasteurized milk that has had a starter introduced to it, will separate into curds and whey when a certain level of acidity is reached. If the whey is drained off, you have curd cheese – it is that simple. Pasteurized milk should *never* be left to sour naturally because it will just go bad rather than ripen.

In cheesemaking, however, it is not always convenient to have coagulation at a very acid level; some cheeses require coagulation while the milk has a low acidity. This is where an enzyme such as rennet comes in. Rennet has two main functions in cheesemaking: to curdle fresh, unripened milk without souring it, thus providing a sweet curd; and, in cheese made from ripened or sour milk, to hasten the solidification process without further altering the acidity. The use of smaller or larger quantities of rennet results in softer or more moist curd; this affects the speed at which the whey drains, which in turn affects the texture and flavour of the cheese.

Rennet works best when the milk is warm and contains soluble calcium. Milk naturally contains calcium in a soluble form, but if it is boiled or heated to a high temperature this chemical element becomes insoluble and the rennet will not work. The action is not reversed when the milk is cooled again; and this explains why you cannot use boiled, sterilized, or ultra-heat-treated ('long-life') milk to make junket or cheese where rennet is employed. The lower the temperature at which the rennet is added, the longer the curd will take to form and the softer the curd will be.

Once coagulated, the firm curd can be eaten as it is, as Little Miss Muffet did when she ate her curds and whey. Alternatively, it can be treated in a variety of ways according to the type of cheese to be made.

The curd is broken or cut to release the whey. Whey consists of mostly water and lactose; the fat and other constituents of milk remain caught in the curd along with the protein. The size of the broken curds regulates the speed at which the whey is released, and this in turn helps to determine the type of cheese that will finally emerge. Generally speaking, the smaller the curds, the quicker the drainage and the harder the cheese. For most soft cheeses, the curds are kept relatively large and the drainage is quite slow.

The whey that is released should be clear and greenish. If the whey is very cloudy, this means that a considerable amount of fat is being lost. This will happen if the curd is treated roughly. Alternatively, it can indicate that the curd has been cut before it has set properly. When ready for cutting, a curd should split cleanly when pressed with a finger.

Cheesemaking should be carried out at a temperature of about 65-70°F (18-21°C); lower temperatures inhibit drainage and the longer the whey remains in the cheese, the more acid the cheese becomes.

Cheese should never be made at the same time as bread or yogurt, or when cooking fruit and there must be no fermenting wine about, as the yeasts react unfavourably on the cheese.

7.
INGREDIENTS

Milk
The milk used for the cheesemaking recipes in this book is pasteurized cow's milk, unless stated differently in the recipe. I use the silver-topped milk delivered by the milkman, or cartoned milk from the shop, but skimmed or partially-skimmed milk can be used if you want to produce a low-fat soft cheese. Milk with a high fat content, such as Jersey and Guernsey, will make a richer cheese, but it is more difficult to work with. It requires more rennet and higher temperatures, so stick to the basic silver-topped milk at first. Do *not* use sterilized or UHT ('long-life') milk for cheese made with rennet; the temperatures used in sterilization and the ultra-heat-treatment are higher than the pasteurization temperature and so cause changes in the milk which affect rennet action. (This is explained on page 118.)

Goat's milk can be used to make any of the cheeses in this book, but the rennet should be added at a slightly lower temperature than when cow's milk is used.

Rennet
According to the English dictionary rennet is 'a substance for coagulating milk'. The word rennet is a derivative of the word rennin. Rennin comes from the stomach of a suckling calf. The enzyme action of rennet causes the milk to curdle, producing the solids that make cheese. Because natural rennet is of animal origin, many vegetarians prefer to use cheese made from non-animal rennet. Vegetarian rennet is made from a microbial enzyme derived from the mould *Mucor miehei* which has the ability

to curdle milk in the same way that animal rennet does. This is available as a liquid (and in tablet form in the USA) and gives excellent results.

Liquid rennet is the easiest form to handle both for measuring and handling. Vegetarian rennet can be obtained from many suppliers (see *Useful Addresses*) and also from health food and wholefood shops. If it is bottled in a dark container to keep out the light and kept in the refrigerator after opening, it will keep for many weeks (even months).

The quantities given in the recipes are for 'Standard Cheese Rennet' (one ml can clot at least 15,000 ml of milk). Junket rennet can be used for some cheeses when a very soft curd is acceptable. However, for most cheeses this is simply not strong enough and a proper cheese rennet must be used. When using Essence of Rennet (or junket rennet) for making soft cheese, the correct usage is approximately ten times as much Essence as Standard Rennet – the container should give details of this. (Junket rennet is normally 10 per cent of the strength of Standard Rennet.) As a general rule one teaspoon (5 ml) of Essence is sufficient for one pint/570 ml/2½ cups milk. Standard Cheese Rennet is *always diluted* with six times its own volume of cooled, boiled water unless stated differently in the recipe.

Cream
Use pasteurized single or double cream depending upon the type of cream cheese you wish to make.

Annatto
Annatto is a natural vegetable colouring which can be used if required to give a reddish or orange colour to the cheese.

Salt
This brings out the flavour of the cheese and also acts as a preservative. Use fine sea salt.

8.
CHEESEMAKING EQUIPMENT

The equipment needed for making soft and semi-hard cheeses is relatively simple, and much of it can be improvised from ordinary kitchen utensils. Special cheesemaking equipment can be added as you progress and your enthusiasm grows! A list of suppliers is given in the appendix on page 157. You will need the following:

Thermometers. A proper dairy thermometer which floats is best but if this is not available an ordinary jam-making thermometer will do, but you will have to hold it, which can be tiring. It must be graduated to 220°F (104°C). In the USA, there are useful clip-on dairy thermometers which can be attached to the side of the container, but I have not seen these anywhere else. A room thermometer is also important, for the ambient temperature does have a marked effect on results.

Spoons, ladles and knives. Apart from teaspoons and table-spoons for measuring the cheese starter, rennet and annatto, you will need a long handled spoon for stirring the milk, a perforated flat ladle or slice (pancake turner), a a soup-type ladle for transferring the curd and a long-bladed palette knife for cutting the curd. Ordinary kitchen utensils are quite sufficient, but they should be of stainless steel.

Mixing bowls. The capacity of these depends on the type of cheese being made and the quantity of milk involved. Ordinary Pyrex (heatproof glass) mixing bowls are suitable. Large stainless steel bowls are a good investment. You will be surprised how useful they are if you do a lot of cooking and preserving.

Buckets. For larger quantities of milk use a 2 gallon (9 litres) capacity bucket. Stainless steel is best – never use galvanised iron, zinc or aluminium as these will corrode. There is a special dairy bucket made of strong plastic which will withstand most of the temperatures used, is easy to sterilize and much cheaper than stainless steel.

Colander. A large colander is essential.

Cheese mats. These are placed on the boards to allow the whey to drain away from the cheese. They should be the same length and width as the boards. Special draining mats, made from wooden reeds which are sewn together with cotton twine, are available from suppliers, but it is possible to use straw or reed table mats provided they are colourfast and that the weave can be scrubbed free of curd particles. If you cannot obtain suitable draining mats, folded cloths can be used.

Cheese cloths. These are squares of cloth used for draining the curds. You can make them yourself from good quality butter muslin bought from any dress fabric shop. A large square, referred to in the recipes, is roughly 18 inches (53 cm) square and of double thickness. You should have five or six if you intend making many cheeses. Cheese cloths should always be boiled for 5 minutes before use. You will also need some odd pieces of string to tie and hang up the muslin draining bags.

Cheese boards. These are used for placing the moulds on while the cheese is draining. They should be of well-seasoned hardwood – about 1 inch (2.5 cm) thick. Wooden chopping-boards of varying sizes can be used provided they are not pitted or scored.

Moulds. These come in various shapes and sizes, details of which are given with the relevant recipes. The best ones are made from stainless steel or food-grade plastic. However, you can improvise quite successfully with round or square bottomless cake tins, or with large coffee tins from which the base has been removed or which have holes pierced in the side. When you punch holes in home-made moulds, remember that they must be punched from the inside out, otherwise you will tear the cheese when trying to get it out. You will find that the moulds made from coffee or tea tins have a very short life as they deteriorate with use, and should therefore be replaced as necessary. Never use plastic piping or any material which might contain toxic resins.

Water bath. The milk should nearly always be heated indirectly in a water bath. The water bath can be an ordinary saucepan provided it is larger than the bowl or pan containing the milk. The water around the inner bath ensures that the milk is heated evenly.

Whey collector. When making soft cheese in moulds there is a lot of free whey. You will need to stand your mould on its drainage board and/or mat in something such as a baking tin or tray to collect the liquid. See page 136 for making whey cheese.

Care and Cleaning of Equipment
Everything you use, including work surfaces, should be thoroughly clean and preferably sterilized. Most home cheesemaking failures are caused by unclean or unsterile equipment. Milk is an ideal medium for the growth of harmful bacteria; all traces of it must be removed from utensils before they are used again.

All utensils that come into contact with milk should be rinsed under cold running water immediately after use (hot water coagulates the milk protein and makes the particles difficult to remove.) Then wash and scrub in hot soapy water. An ordinary kitchen liquid detergent, or alternatively washing soda crystals, can be used. Rinse thoroughly in clean hot water. Finally, sterilize the equipment in one of three ways:

1. Immerse the equipment completely in boiling water for up to five minutes.

2. Steam utensils for a minimum of five minutes in a large saucepan with about 2 inches (5 cm) of boiling water in the bottom and a tight-fitting lid on top. Wooden items such as cheese boards and mats should be boiled or steamed for at least 20 minutes. Remember that you cannot boil or steam plastic or polythene equipment.

3. Immerse the equipment in a solution of household bleach (sodium hypochlorite), by diluting 1 fluid oz (2 tablespoons) of bleach in 1 gallon (9 litres) cold water. Rinse the utensils thoroughly with clean cold water to remove any traces of the hypochlorite which might otherwise interfere with the cheesemaking bacteria. Leave the utensils to drain dry, and store them carefully in a clean place. Just before using them again, all utensils should be resterilized.

A dilute solution of hypochlorite can also be used for wiping down work surfaces.

9.
CHEESEMAKING RECIPES

FLAVOUR VARIATIONS

Soft cheese can be infinitely varied. Here are some ideas. Others will no doubt occur to you.

1. Shape a small cheese, then roll it in sweet paprika, mixed fresh herbs (such as parsley, savory, marjoram or thyme) with garlic, crushed green peppercorns, chopped nuts, toasted oatmeal or sesame seeds until well coated.

2. Mix some dried fruits and /or honey into the cheese before you shape it.

3. Soak raisins in dark rum then press the swollen raisins into the cheese.

RENNET-CURD CHEESE

(Makes about 4oz/100g/½ cup cheese)

Basic milk cheese

Imperial (Metric)	American
1 pint (570 ml) whole or skimmed milk	2½ cups whole or skimmed milk
1 teaspoon vegetarian junket rennet (also known as Essence of Rennet)	1 teaspoon vegetarian junket rennet (also known as Essence of Rennet)

1. Pour the milk into a double saucepan, or alternatively into a bowl standing in a pan of simmering water, and heat gently until a temperature of 110°F (43°C) is reached on a thermometer.

2. Remove the top saucepan or bowl from the hot water. Stir in the junket rennet (N.B. *not* cheese rennet). Leave it to cool at room temperature while the rennet clots the milk – about 2 hours.

3. Line a colander or sieve with a square of scalded muslin (cheesecloth) and stand over a bowl. Turn the junket into it. Gather up the corners of the cloth, tie them together to form a bag, and hang it up to drain.

4. After 6-8 hours, open the bag, scrape the curd from the sides of the cloth. Mix the firm curd with the softer curd in the centre, and re-hang the bag. Repeat this process after another 6-8 hours if the cheese is still wetter than you want it.

5. When the cheese has the texture you want, work in a little salt if desired, turn it into a bowl, cover and refrigerate. Alternatively, form into a pat for immediate use. Use as a low-fat soft cheese.

COTTAGE CHEESE

(Makes 8oz/225g/1 cup)

Imperial (Metric)	American
2 pints (1.12 litres) skimmed or whole milk	5 cups skimmed or whole milk
1 tablespoon cultured buttermilk or natural yogurt (optional)	1 tablespoon cultured buttermilk or plain yogurt (optional)
2 teaspoons vegetarian junket rennet	2 teaspoons vegetarian junket rennet

1. Heat the milk gradually to 100°F (38°C) and stir in the starter, if using, and the rennet. Cover and leave, undisturbed in a warm place, to coagulate – up to 2 hours.

2. When the curd has set, cut into ½ inch (1 cm) cubes with a knife; cut it vertically and then turn the curd over carefully with a spoon and cut it the other way.

3. Slowly re-heat the curd to 100°F (38°C), stirring all the time to keep it from sticking together. Remove from the heat and allow to stand for 15 minutes.

4. Line a colander with a square of scalded muslin (cheese-cloth) and stand it over a bowl. Ladle in the curds and leave to drain for about 10 minutes. Hold the colander under a running, cold water tap, and literally 'wash' the curds, to rinse off the whey. This process produces the traditional lumpy texture associated with cottage cheese. Stand the colander over a bowl and leave to drain for a few minutes.

5. Put the drained curds into a bowl. For a richer flavour, the cottage cheese may be 'creamed' by mixing in a little single (light) cream or yogurt depending on taste. It may also be salted and any flavouring added at this stage. Home-made cottage cheese does not contain preservatives, so does not keep as long as the commercial variety. Keep in the refrigerator and eat within 2-3 days.

LACTIC CURD CHEESE

(Makes 2-2½ lb/1 kg/2-2½ pounds of cheese)

This is an unrenneted soft cheese with endless possibilities. The quantities given in this recipe may be halved or quartered and the finished cheese may be flavoured in a variety of ways. You can add chopped garlic and mixed herbs, grated lemon rind, caraway seeds, or crushed green peppercorns. A small cheese shaped into a neat round or cylinder may be rolled in paprika, toasted oatmeal, cracked black peppercorns or wrapped in vine leaves. The unflavoured curd may, of course, be used in any of the recipes calling for curd cheese in this book. You can if you wish use skimmed milk to make a low-fat curd cheese.

Imperial (Metric)	American
1 gallon (4.5 litres) milk	20 cups milk
2 tablespoons cultured buttermilk	2 tablespoons cultured buttermilk

1. Pour the milk into a stainless steel bowl or enamelled pan and set it into a larger pan of simmering water. Slowly heat the milk to 75°F (24°C) and add the buttermilk. Stir deeply and thoroughly, cover the container and leave, undisturbed, at a room temperature of 65°-70°F (18°-21°C) for 12 hours or until the milk has coagulated. This can take up to 24 hours.

2. When the curd is firm enough to pass the 'clean finger' test (see note below), line a colander with a large square of dry muslin (cheesecloth) and stand it over a bowl to catch the whey.

3. Carefully ladle the curd on to the muslin (cheesecloth) then pull up the corners of the cloth and tie them tightly; hang up the resulting bag to drain. For best results, allow 36-48 hours' drainage in a temperature of 65°-70°F (18°-21°C). If you wish the cheese to drain more quickly, open the cloth at 3-4 hourly intervals, scraping down the curd on the outside of the cloth and mixing it well with the softer curd in the middle. The cloth can also be changed.

4. Put the curds in a bowl, salt to taste, and mix in herbs if desired. Beating will make it creamier in texture.

Note: If a finger inserted into the curd comes out clean, the curd is firm enough.

BUTTERMILK CURD CHEESE
(Makes about 8oz/225g/1 cup)

Imperial (Metric)	American
2 pints (1.12 litres) cultured buttermilk	5 cups cultured buttermilk

1. Pour the buttermilk into a double saucepan, or alternatively into a bowl standing in a saucepan of simmering water, and heat slowly to 160°F (71°C), stirring occasionally. The heat will cause the curds to separate from the whey. Remove from the heat, cover and leave for about 2 hours to allow the curds to settle.

2. Tip the curds into a colander or sieve lined with a large square of scalded muslin (cheesecloth), tie it up with string to form a bag, then hang it over a bowl and leave it to drain for 1½-2 hours – the longer it is left the drier the curds will be.

3. Scrape the curds into a bowl and, if desired, add sea salt and herbs to taste.

Note: This cheese will have a granular, spreadable texture, and a slightly acid taste. Serve with salads, jacket potatoes and so on, or mix with mayonnaise and use as a sandwich spread.

SINGLE-CREAM CHEESE

(Makes about 4oz/100g/½ cup)

Imperial (Metric)	American
1 pint (570 ml) single cream	2½ cups light cream
1 teaspoon cultured buttermilk	1 teaspoon cultured buttermilk
¼ teaspoon vegetarian cheese rennet	¼ teaspoon vegetarian cheese rennet

1. Gently heat the cream to 75°F (24°C) and add the buttermilk. Cover the bowl and leave for 2-3 hours to allow the cream to ripen.

2. Add the rennet diluted with six times its own volume of cold boiled water, stirring well to mix. Cover and leave in a warm place for 8-12 hours or until the cream coagulates. A temperature range of 70°-80°F (21°-27°C) is ideal.

3. Ladle the coagulum in slices into a thick cloth (2 cheese cloths put together work very well) which has been scalded and cooled before use. Tie the four corners of the cloth with string and hang the bag in a cool (50°-55°F, 10°-13°C) well-ventilated room to drain. Alternatively, the bag of curd can be placed horizontally between two cheese boards on a draining rack with a 1-2 pound (0.5-1 kilo) weight on top. This will speed up the draining process.

4. Every four to eight hours, scrape the harder curd from the cloth and mix it with the softer curd in the middle. The more often this is done the quicker the cheese will drain. If the cloth becomes clogged with curd drainage will be restricted. The cloth should be changed at intervals.

5. When sufficiently drained the curd will have a thick, rather grainy consistency. Add salt and herbs if desired. The cheese can be shaped into a neat round or roll and wrapped in greaseproof paper or foil, or packed into plastic cartons. Store in the refrigerator and eat within 2-3 days.

DOUBLE-CREAM CHEESE

(Makes about 4oz/100g/½ cup)

This uses the same proportions of cream and buttermilk as the recipe for single-cream cheese but it is neither ripened nor renneted.

Imperial (Metric)	American
1 pint (570 ml) double cream	2½ cups heavy cream
1 teaspoon cultured buttermilk	1 teaspoon cultured buttermilk
1 teaspoon sea salt	1 teaspoon sea salt

1. Heat the cream to 75°F (24°C), add the buttermilk and salt, stirring in well. Salting the cream at this stage helps it to drain well and improves its keeping quality.

2. Cover and leave in a warm place to coagulate as before. Ladle it into a thick cloth and hang it up to drain in a cool place. The treatment during and after draining should be the same as for single-cream cheese, but with even more care, in view of its cost.

TUMA – EWE'S MILK CHEESE

(Makes about 2 pounds/1 kilo)

This is my mother's recipe for a sheep milk cheese and Ricotta from Sicily. The whey produced as a by-product of the *tuma* is used to make the Ricotta or 're-cooked' cheese. Both these cheeses are traditionally made using wicker baskets instead of moulds, giving the cheese a beautiful design. *Tuma* is the firm young cheese which becomes Pecorino after 3 months of maturity. If a pepper cheese is desired, black peppercorns may be mixed with the cheese to produce Pecorino Pepato. Once matured the cheese may be grated and used in place of Parmesan cheese. I buy ewe's milk frozen in 1 pint (570 ml) packets from my local wholefood shop.

Imperial (Metric)	American
1 gallon (4.5 litres) unpasteurized ewe's milk	20 cups unpasteurized ewe's milk
½ teaspoon vegetarian cheese rennet	½ teaspoon vegetarian cheese rennet

1. Empty all except 1 pint (570 ml or 2½ cups) of the milk into a large pan. Slowly heat the milk to 95°F (35°C), add the rennet diluted in three times its own volume of cool, boiled water and stir in thoroughly. Cover and leave for half an hour, undisturbed by draughts or vibration. To test the curd, touch it with the back of a finger. If your finger comes away clean, the curd is ready.

2. Stir gently to break up the curd, then put on a low heat for a minute or two, stirring occasionally. Take off the heat and drain off most of the whey into a bowl, keeping it clean as it is used for the Ricotta.

3. Place two flat sticks across the pan as a support for the cheese basket. Take handfuls of curd and squeeze out the surplus liquid before packing it into the basket. When the basket is full press down to expel further the liquid. Empty the pressed curd from the basket into one hand (it should all adhere nicely in its shape), change into the other hand and replace it upside down in the basket. While it drains make the Ricotta.

4. Return the rest of the whey to the pan and heat to just below boiling point, then add the pint of milk that was set aside earlier. Watch the whey very carefully, stirring all the time. Do not let the liquid boil. Soon the albumin, helped by the casein in the milk, will begin to flocculate and appear as a creamy white foam on the surface. This is Ricotta. Keep skimming this off into a finer wicker basket or a sieve lined with a square of scalded muslin (cheesecloth). The Ricotta will not keep any longer than fresh milk but it is delicious eaten with a sprinkling of chopped fresh herbs with bread, or as a dessert with fruit such as strawberries.

5. Having made the Ricotta, return now to the true cheese. Put the basket with its contents, into the hot whey, the heat forming the rind. Lift out, turn the cheese in the basket as before and immerse again, and finally lift out to drain. When quite cold, lightly salt the top of the cheese, leave overnight in the basket. Next day, take the cheese out of the basket and salt the remaining surfaces. Put on a wooden cheese board and turn daily for about a week. You can start eating the cheese at this stage or let it mature for a little while longer.

Note: In other parts of Italy and in the United States, the word *tuma* is used to describe fresh cheese made by Italians made from cow's milk and is sometimes called 'basket cheese'.

WHEY CURD CHEESE

(Makes about 12oz/340g/1½ cups)

Imperial (Metric)	American
1 pint (570 ml) fresh whey	2½ cups fresh whey
2 pints (1.12 litres) milk	5 cups milk
Sea salt to taste	Sea salt to taste

1. Pour the whey into a pan – the exact quantity is really irrelevant providing that the 1:2 (whey to milk) ratio is observed – and heat very slowly until the surface looks frothy, then pour in the milk. Continue heating for 5 minutes or so, stirring all the time. Keep the heat turned down low, as the liquid must not boil.

2. When it starts to curdle, take the pan off the heat, cover and leave undisturbed for about 2 hours, then pour it into a muslin-lined colander. Hang up the muslin bag and drain for 2-3 hours. Add salt to taste, then pack it into a plastic container. Store in the refrigerator and eat within 2-3 days.

YOGURT CHEESE *Method I*

(Makes 6-8 oz/175-225g/¾-1 cup cheese)

Imperial (Metric)	American
1 pint (570 ml) natural yogurt, home-made or shop bought	2½ cups plain yogurt, home-made or store bought

1. Line a colander or sieve with a square of scalded muslin (cheesecloth), with enough over the edges to gather up, and stand over a bowl to catch the whey.

2. Pour or spoon in the yogurt, gather up the corners of the cloth, tie them together to form a bag and hang it up to drain for 12-24 hours. Most of the whey drains quickly in the first eight hours, after that there is very slow loss – obviously, the longer the cheese is left to drain the firmer it will become (and the less it will weigh!)

3. When it has the texture you want, work in a little salt if desired, turn the cheese into a bowl and refrigerate. Eat within a few days. Use as a low-fat soft cheese.

Note: Some commercially-made yogurt is suitable for making into soft cheese but only if it is the natural unstirred variety, therefore the label should be checked carefully. Best results will be obtained with home-made yogurt.

The whey can be used in breadmaking or soups and casseroles. Straight from the refrigerator it makes a refreshing summer drink.

YOGURT CHEESE *Method II*

(Makes 4oz/100g/½ cup cheese)

Imperial (Metric)	American
1 pint (570 ml) natural yogurt, home-made or shop bought	2½ cups plain yogurt, home-made or store bought

1. Place the yogurt in a double saucepan and heat to 100°F (38°C), when it should separate into curds and whey.

2. Line a colander or sieve with a square of scalded muslin (cheesecloth) and stand over a bowl. Pour the curdled yogurt into it. Gather up the corners of the cloth and tie with a piece of string.

3. Leave to drain for about an hour, then untie the cloth and scrape the resulting cheese into a bowl. Mix in a little salt if desired. Store in the refrigerator until consumed.

Note: Vary the fresh sharp flavour of yogurt cheese by beating in chopped chives, raw onion, crushed garlic, or any herbs of choice.

YOGURT CHEESE ROLL

Imperial (Metric)	American
1 pint (570 ml) natural yogurt, preferably home-made	2½ cups plain yogurt, preferably home-made
Sea salt and freshly ground black pepper	Sea salt and freshly ground black pepper
2 teaspoons olive oil	2 teaspoons olive oil
1 teaspoon dried thyme, or any herb of choice	1 teaspoon dried thyme, or any herb of choice
2 teaspoons sesame seeds	2 teaspoons sesame seeds

1. Line a colander or sieve with a square of muslin (cheesecloth) which has been boiled for 5 minutes and then cooled. Stand it over a bowl.

2. Pour or spoon the yogurt into the muslin (cheesecloth) and tie it up with string so that it forms a bag. Lift it out of the colander. Hang it over a bowl or over the sink and leave to drain overnight.

3. The next day, turn the drained curds into a bowl and beat with a wooden spoon until smooth, adding a little salt, pepper and the olive oil. Form it into a cylinder shape and chill till firm.

4. Pound the dried thyme and sesame seeds together in a mortar, then tip them on to a piece of greaseproof or non-stick paper. Roll the cheese into it until it is coated all over, including the round ends. Chill in the refrigerator until required. Serve cut into slices, with wholemeal bread or toast.

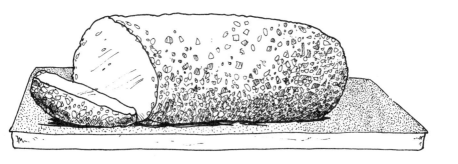

LEMON CHEESE (Acid-curd cheese)

(Makes about 6-8oz/175-225g/¾-1 cup)

Imperial (Metric)	American
2 pints (1.12 litres) milk	5 cups milk
Juice of 2 lemons	Juice of 2 lemons
Sea salt to taste	Sea salt to taste

1. Heat the milk to 100°F (38°C) in a double saucepan or a bowl standing in a saucepan of simmering water. Remove from the heat and stir in the lemon juice. Leave the curds to settle for 15 minutes.

2. Line a colander or sieve with a square of scalded muslin (cheesecloth) and place over a bowl to catch the whey. Ladle the curds into the muslin (cheesecloth) with a perforated ladle or spoon. Then gather the corners of the cloth together and tie with a piece of string. Hang the bag over a bowl and leave for one hour or until the curds have stopped dripping.

3. Remove the cheese from the cloth, scraping it off the sides if necessary, and add salt to taste. The cheese is now ready to eat. It has a moist, spreadable texture and a very pleasant slightly lemon taste. The whey can be used in baking or served as a cold drink.

PANIR

(Makes about 8oz/225g/1 cup)

An Indian firm curd cheese, using cream of tartar to curdle the milk.

Imperial (Metric)	American
½ level teaspoon cream of tartar	½ level teaspoon cream of tartar
½ breakfast cup hot water	½ breakfast cup hot water
2 pints (1.12 litres) milk	5 cups milk

1. Dissolve the cream of tartar in the cup of hot water.

2. Bring the milk to the boil, remove from the heat, stir in the tartaric acid liquid, then continue stirring until all the milk curdles. Leave aside for 15 minutes.

3. Line a colander with a square of scalded muslin (cheese-cloth), with enough over the edges to gather up, and stand over a bowl.

4. Gather up the corners of the cloth together, tie securely and hang up to drain for 30 minutes.

5. Place the curds, still wrapped in the cloth, between two cheese boards and weight down with a weight of about 5 pounds (2.25 kilos). Leave for 2-2½ hours. Strip off the muslin (cheesecloth) and cut into cubes.

LACTIC GOAT'S CHEESE

(Makes 4oz/100g/½ cup cheese)

Imperial (Metric)	American
1 pint (570 ml) goat's milk	2½ cups goat's milk
1 teaspoon lactic acid	1 teaspoon lactic acid

1. Pour the milk into a double saucepan, or alternatively into a bowl standing in a pan of simmering water, and heat until a temperature of 102°F (40°C) is reached on a thermometer.

2. Remove the top saucepan or bowl from the hot water and stir in the lactic acid.

3. Allow to settle for 20 minutes before spooning the curds into a colander or sieve lined with a square of scalded muslin (cheesecloth). Gather up the corners of the cloth, tie them together to form a bag, and hang it up to drain for about an hour.

4. Remove the cheese from the cloth; you may have to scrape it off the sides with a spoon. Turn it into a bowl, add a little salt, pepper and freshly chopped herbs of choice. Form into a flat round shape, then cover the outside with coarsely crushed black peppercorns. Chill in the refrigerator before serving.

Note: Bottles of lactic acid are available from any good chemist (druggist).

COULOMMIERS-TYPE CHEESE

The traditional mould for Coulommiers cheese consists of two stainless steel hoops which fit into each other. The assembled hoops are 6 inches (15 cm) in height and 4¾ inches (12 cm) in diameter. They are filled with curd, and once it sinks below the level of the top hoop, the top hoop is removed and the cheese is turned over. If the Coulommiers mould were not in two sections, the cheese would splatter when turned over in the tall mould. Home-made moulds can be made from two tins with the same dimensions and both ends removed. These can be sellotaped together for the early draining process. This recipe will make three cheeses about 4 inches (10 cm) in diameter and 1½ inches (4 cm) high. If you use 4 pints/2.24 litres/10 cups of milk you can make two slightly smaller cheeses, but remember that all the other ingredients will have to be adjusted in proportion.

Imperial (Metric)	American
1 gallon (4.5 litres) milk	20 cups milk
2 tablespoons cultured buttermilk	2 tablespoons cultured buttermilk
1 teaspoon vegetarian cheese rennet	1 teaspoon vegetarian cheese rennet
Sea salt	Sea salt

1. Pour the milk into a double saucepan, or alternatively into a bowl standing in a pan of simmering water, and heat gently until it reaches a temperature of 90°F (32°C). Add the cultured buttermilk and stir well. Dilute the rennet in six time its own volume of cooled, boiled water and mix into the warm milk.

2. Deep-stir for a couple of minutes, then cover and leave at room temperature 65°-75°F (18°-24°C) for 1-1½ hours, or until a firm curd forms. To test the curd, touch it with the back of a finger. If your finger comes away clean, the curd is ready. (If not ready, leave the curd a little longer.)

3. Meanwhile, sterilize three Coulommiers moulds, three cheese draining mats, three cheese boards and a perforated flat ladle. Place the mats on the boards and place the moulds on the mats. Stand the assembled equipment in a tray or shallow baking tin.

4. Make an imprint with the top of the mould into the surface of the curd. Scoop out this piece of curd and slide it onto a clean plate or saucer; make one for every cheese. These are to make neat tops for your cheeses.

5. Then using the perforated flat ladle, cut thin slices from the curd and gently lower them into the bottom of the moulds. Try to avoid breaking the curd, as this will result in a loss of fat and a tough, dry cheese. It is best to fill all the moulds at the same time so that the curd is evenly distributed between them and you will finish with cheeses of the same size. The thinner you slice the curd, the faster the cheese will drain.

6. Continue filling the moulds until the curd reaches the top, then leave for a few minutes for some of the whey to drain off and for the curds to sink in the moulds; ladle in more curd until you have used it all. Now slide on the 'tops'. Be careful not to knock the moulds or you will find the curd shoots out! Cover the moulds with muslin (cheesecloth) and leave to drain for 9 hours or overnight. Keep the cheese in a room with a constant temperature, preferably 70°F (21°C).

7. When the curd has sunk below the level of the top hoop, remove the hoop and place a freshly sterilized draining mat and board on the top of each mould. Carefully lift the mould and cheese boards between two hands and quickly turn the cheese over. (This is rather like turning out a cake.) Then take away the old board and gently remove the mat, making sure not to tear the cheese, which may be sticking to it. Remember to clean and sterilize the old mat and board immediately after use.

8. Repeat this process twice a day for the next two days, by which time the cheeses should be firm enough to hold their shapes and the moulds can be removed. Sprinkle salt on the tops and bottoms of the cheeses and rub gently in. Lightly wrap in greaseproof paper and refrigerate for 24 hours before eating.

HERBED COULOMMIERS CHEESE

As the curds are ladled into the mould fresh herbs, or freshly ground black pepper, may be sprinkled between the slices of curd. A tasty combination is to add a clove of finely chopped garlic with a tablespoon of freshly chopped parsley. Alternatively, try a sprinkling of cayenne pepper.

Note: The curd may take up to 24 hours longer to drain, depending on the weather.

COLWICK CHEESE

(Makes 2 cheeses)

Colwick is an English soft cheese which takes its name from the village of Colwick near Nottingham. This is a round cheese with a hollow centre, and is unusual in that it is traditionally served as a dessert with its hollow filled with fresh fruit and whipped cream. Colwick cheese was traditionally made in a single perforated mould about 7 inches (18 cm) high and 5 inches (12.5 cm) in diameter. However, the moulds are no longer available and Coulommiers moulds can be used instead. If improvised moulds are used, the base of the tin should be cut away and holes pierced in the sides.

Imperial (Metric)	American
1 gallon (4.5 litres) milk	20 cups milk
1 dessertspoon cultured buttermilk	2 teaspoons cultured buttermilk
1½ teaspoons vegetarian cheese rennet	1½ teaspoons vegetarian cheese rennet

1. Pour the milk into a double saucepan, or alternatively into a bowl standing in a pan of simmering water, and heat gently until it reaches a temperature of 90°F (32°C). Remove from the heat, add the cultured buttermilk and stir in well. Dilute the rennet in six times its own volume of cooled, boiled water and mix into the warm milk. Top-stir (i.e. just the top ½ inch/1 cm) for a couple of minutes, to prevent all the cream from rising, then cover and leave undisturbed in a warm place for 1-1½ hours or until a firm curd forms.

2. Meanwhile, sterilize two moulds, two cheese draining mats, two cheese boards and a perforated flat ladle. Place the mats on the boards and place the moulds on the mats. Line the moulds with previously boiled muslin (cheesecloth), letting it hang over the edges. Stand the whole lot in a tray or shallow baking tin.

3. Using the perforated flat ladle, transfer the curd in thin slices into the cloth lined moulds.

4. After an hour or so, pull the muslin (cheesecloth) upwards and inwards drawing the curd from the sides of the mould. Take three corners of the muslin (cheesecloth) and tie together with the fourth. Leave the knot centrally placed on the surface of the curd. Repeat the process several times during the next few hours, to produce the curled-over edges and a depression in the middle.

5. Allow to drain for 24 to 36 hours when it should be firm enough to handle. Remove the mould and peel off the muslin (cheesecloth) carefully. Fill the centres just before serving.

CAERPHILLY-STYLE CHEESE
(Makes one cheese weighing 2¼-2½ lb/1.012-1.125 kg)

Imperial (Metric)	American
2 gallons (9 litres) milk	40 cups milk
1½ fl oz (42 ml) cultured buttermilk	3 tablespoons cultured buttermilk
1½ teaspoons vegetarian cheese rennet	1½ teaspoons vegetarian cheese rennet
1 oz (25g) sea salt	1 ounce sea salt
1-2 oz (25-50g) hard vegetable fat	1-2 ounces hard vegetable fat

1. Pour the milk into a stainless steel or white plastic dairy bucket and heat to 90°F (32°C). This can be done by placing the bucket in a sink of hot water and stirring the milk until the correct temperature is reached. Take the bucket out of the hot water, otherwise the temperature of the milk will continue to rise. Add the cultured buttermilk, and then cover and leave to ripen for 30 minutes.

2. Add the rennet diluted in six times its own volume of cooled, boiled water. Deep-stir for one minute, and then top-stir (i.e. just the top ½ inch/1 cm) until coagulation begins. (You can tell when coagulation is beginning because the curd will tend to cling to your spoon as you take it out of the milk). Cover and leave for 45 minutes, or until a firm curd forms.

3. Using a palette knife, cut the curd into ½ inch (1 cm) strips. Then cut at right angles to these strips to form ½ inch (1 cm) columns of curd. Next, using a perforated flat ladle, lower this into the curd and make horizontal cuts at ½ inch (1 cm) depths, all the way to the bottom of the bucket.

4. Stand the bucket in a sink of hot water and quickly raise the temperature to 92°F (33°C). Keep the curd at this temperature for 40 minutes, stirring all the time to prevent the curd pieces from sticking together. To test whether the curd is ready, take a small piece and press it with your fingers. If your fingerprint remains the curd is ready, if it does not, keep stirring at the same temperature until it does – it merely means that the acidity is only developing slowly.

5. Leave the curd to 'pitch' (i.e. settle in the bottom of the bucket in the whey) for 5 minutes then pour off as much whey as you can. (Avoid leaving the curds in the whey too long otherwise too much acidity will develop for this type of cheese.) Pile the curds on one side of the bucket, leave for 5 minutes, then pour off any more whey if possible. This is made easier if you tip the bucket slightly. Cut the curd into cubes, leave 10 minutes, and again tilt off any free whey.

6. Turn the curds into a large colander lined with a square of scalded muslin (cheesecloth) and stand it in the sink or draining board. Gather up the corners of the cloth and transfer the curd to a scale – there should be about 3½-4 pounds (1.5-1.8 kg.) If your bag of curd weighs considerably more, go on draining it.

7. Return the curds, still in the cloth, to the colander in the sink, break into walnut-sized pieces and mix in the salt.

8. Line the mould with damp muslin (cheesecloth) and pack in the curd as evenly as possible. (A 6 or 7 inch (15 or 17½ cm) diameter cake tin with its base removed and holes drilled in the sides will serve in lieu of a proper mould.) Fold the cloth over the curd, and place the follower on top (i.e. a piece of thick wood that fits inside the mould). However, if using a cake tin, the removed base will suffice. Put 4 pounds (1.8 kg.) of weights on top. Remove after 10 minutes, then turn and repeat twice more at 10 minute intervals. Leave the cheese under the weights for 14-16 hours.

9. Take the cheese out of the mould, unwrap, and dry with a clean cloth. Brush the surface of the cheese with a thin layer of melted fat and bandage with butter muslin. Cut 2 circles ½ inch (1 cm) larger than the top and bottom of the cheese and a band which is as wide as the cheese is deep and one and half times its circumference in length.

10. Store the cheese on a shelf (so that the air can circulate around it) in a cool, dry room at a temperature of 50°-60°F (10°-16°C) for two weeks to ripen; remember to turn it daily.

CAMEMBERT-TYPE CHEESE

(Makes 1 cheese)

To make an authentic starter for a traditional white moulded cheese such as Camembert, dissolve a small piece of shop-bought cheese, cut from just under the rind where the flavour is at its strongest, in 2-3 tablespoons of boiled water, which has been cooled to 80°F (27°C). Strain through muslin (cheesecloth) or a tea strainer so that any remaining solid lumps can be discarded. The resulting liquid is now ready to be used as a starter for your cheese.

A Camembert mould usually measures about 5 inches (12.5 cm) in diameter, and 5 inches (12.5 cm) in height. However, an old coffee tin, with both ends removed and holes drilled in the sides, will suffice.

Imperial (Metric)	American
4 pints (2 litres) milk	10 cups milk
2 tablespoons of home-made starter (as previously described)	2 tablespoons of home-made starter (as previously described)
½ teaspoon of vegetarian cheese rennet	½ teaspoon vegetarian cheese rennet
Sea salt	Sea salt

1. Heat the milk in a double saucepan or in a bowl standing in a pan of simmering water to 86°F (30°C), add the starter culture and stir in well. Cover and leave the milk to ripen for 15 minutes.

2. Re-heat the milk to 86°F (30°C), then remove from the heat and add the rennet diluted in four times its own volume of cooled, boiled water. Stir thoroughly. Cover the container and leave undisturbed until a firm curd forms – about 1-1½ hours. Test the curd by laying the back of a finger on it. If the curd does not stick to the finger, the curd is ready. (If not ready, leave the curd a little longer.)

3. Meanwhile, sterilize a mould, a cheese draining mat, a cheese board and a perforated flat ladle. Place the cheese mat on the board and place the mould on top. Stand in a tray or shallow baking tin to catch the whey. (Alternatively, place a piece of folded muslin/cheese-

cloth on a wire cooling rack and place the mould on top. All the equipment should of course be sterilized before it is used.)

4. Using the perforated ladle, transfer the curd into the mould in thin slices. (Keep a firm grip on the mould or the curds will shoot out at the bottom.) The mould can be topped up as the curd sinks.

5. When the curd has sunk halfway down the mould, place a clean mat and board (or freshly boiled muslin/cheesecloth on a wire cooling rack) on top of the mould and carefully turn the whole thing over.

6. Sprinkle the surface of the cheese with a little salt, and turn thrice daily for the next two days. When the cheese is firm and dry, remove its mould and leave it to ripen in a dry, airy place with a temperature of 59°F (15°C) until a white mould starts to form. Then store in a cool, dark place, ideally with a temperature of 55°F (13°C) until ripe, 2 to 6 weeks. Alternatively, if you do not want to wait for the cheese to ripen, it can be eaten in its fresh state.

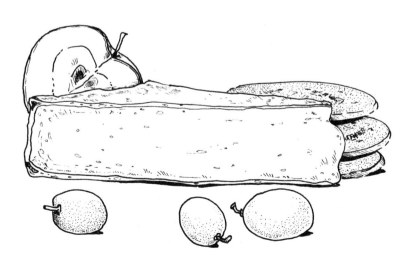

CAMBRIDGE CHEESE (also known as York)

This is a mildly acid soft cheese with a characteristic orange stripe running through the middle. The traditional moulds were rectangular and made in two parts; the top portion was about 8 inches (20 cm) long, 5 inches (12.5 cm) wide and 6 inches (15 cm) deep, and was placed in a shallow tray holding a fitted piece of straw mat. The cheese was served on its own straw mat. These moulds are no longer available, but you can improvise with square or rectangular cake tins with the bottoms cut out. Square cake tins 6 x 6 inches (15 x 15 cm) are ideal, and can be placed directly onto a straw draining mat or a pad of folded muslin (cheesecloth) without the traditional tray.

These cheeses are known as Cambridge or York because they were sold in markets around Ely as well as all over Yorkshire. This quantity of milk will make two cheeses weighing ¾-1 pound (350-450g) each; you can, if you wish, halve the amount to make one cheese.

Imperial (Metric)	American
1½ gallons (7 litres) milk	30 cups milk
1 tablespoon cultured buttermilk	1 tablespoon cultured buttermilk
1½ teaspoons vegetarian cheese rennet	1½ teaspoons vegetarian cheese rennet
1 teaspoon annatto	1 teaspoon annatto

1. Heat the milk to 90°F (32°C). Add the cultured buttermilk and the rennet diluted in six times its own volume of cooled, boiled water. Stir in well for a minute or two then transfer 4 pints (2.24 litres)/10 cups of this to a sterilized bowl and colour it with the annatto. Do not top-stir the remaining milk as this cheese should have a creamy top. Cover both containers and leave for 1 to 1½ hours or until a firm curd forms.

2. Meanwhile, sterilize two moulds, two straw or plastic draining mats and two cheese boards. Place the moulds on a mat and board and stand all this in a tray or shallow baking tin.

3. Cut 'tops' for the cheeses by pressing the moulds into the surface of the white curd. Carefully remove these with a cooking slice (pancake turner) and keep them on plates.

4. Ladle thin slices of the white curd into each mould until about two-thirds full. Divide the orange curd between the two moulds and then finish off with the remaining white curd before positioning the creamy tops into place. This should get the stripe in the middle of the drained cheese. If the moulds are full before all this can be done, simply wait for a few minutes for some of the whey to drain off and the curds to sink in the moulds.

5. Cover with greaseproof paper and leave to drain for 2-3 days until the cheese is about 2 inches (5 cm) high and fairly firm. Do not turn or add any salt. Remove from the moulds. Wrap carefully in greaseproof paper and put in the refrigerator. The cheese is ready to eat in 12 hours and should be eaten within a week. Traditionally this cheese is cut into three portions to show the stripe and the cream.

Glossary

ACID CURD. Curd formed by the natural action of bacteria or by adding an acid to fresh, sweet milk, e.g. lemon juice or vinegar.

ACIDITY. The amount of acid in the milk, the milk's sourness. Acidity is an important element in cheesemaking and it is produced by the cheese starter culture bacteria.

ALBUMIN. A water-soluble protein, a component of whey which coagulates when heat is applied.

ANNATTO. A natural vegetable extract used to give a reddish or orange colour to cheese. This colouring matter is obtained from the pulp which surrounds the seeds of *Bixa ovellana*.

BUTTERFAT. The fat content (cream) in milk.

CASEIN. The major protein of milk which solidifies and precipitates when rennet is added or the milk becomes very acid.

COAGULATE. To clot or solidify.

COAGULUM. The solid product of coagulation.

CURD. The solid matter or coagulum resulting from the formation of lactic acid in, or addition of rennet to, milk.

CURDLE. To cause the proteins in the milk to solidify in an irregular manner.

CULTURED BUTTERMILK. Buttermilk is the by-product of churning cream to make butter. Buttermilk from raw cream will thicken naturally, because of bacterial action. The cultured buttermilk that is available commercially used to be made from buttermilk, but now most of it is made from skimmed milk. A bacterial culture is added and the milk incubated until the desired acidity is reached. Cultured buttermilk contains a bacterial culture similar to that in a cheese starter.

DEEP-STIR. This means to stir right to the bottom of the container in wide circles.

FLOCCULATE. The formation of clouds of coagulated albumin as the result of applying heat to whey. This flocculated protein is the basis for making Ricotta.

FREEZE-DRIED CULTURE. A culture which has been frozen and then heated in a vacuum so that the ice formed on freezing evaporates directly as vapour without turning back into moisture. It is reactivated when added to liquid milk.

HOMOGENIZATION. A process in which the fat globules in whole milk are broken down to smaller particles and evenly distributed so that the cream no longer rises to the surface. The disintegration of the fat globules does make the milk more easily digestible but also makes it unsuitable for cheese-making.

LACTIC ACID. This forms naturally in milk as it sours but the formation is arrested by pasteurization. Lactic acid can be bought in bottles from a chemist (druggist), and can be used to reactivate the souring process.

LACTOSE. The sugar naturally present in milk.

PASTEURIZATION. A mild heat treatment – the milk is heated to 160°F (71°C) for 15 seconds and then cooled rapidly. This not only kills harmful bacteria, but also kills bacteria which would help in natural curd formation.

PITCH. To allow the curd to settle in the whey.

RAW MILK. Milk which is taken fresh from the animal and has not been subjected to any treatment for the removal or control of bacteria and so contains its full quota of naturally-occurring bacteria.

RENNET CURD. The curd formed when rennet is added to milk.

SKIMMED MILK. Milk from which all or some of the cream has been removed. It is obtained by standing the whole milk overnight and ladling off the cream, or by putting it into a centrifugal separator which works instantly.

STARTER. A bacterial culture added to the milk in the early stages of cheesemaking to change the milk sugar (lactose) into lactic acid, and also to contribute to the flavour of the cheese. Commercial cheese starters are available but are quite expensive for the home cheese-maker. Good results are obtained by using cultured butter-milk. In the recipes in this book which use buttermilk, a starter can be substituted in a similar quantity.

STERILIZED MILK. The milk is homogenized, bottled and sealed, and then heat-treated to above boiling point – not less than 212°F (100°C) for 20-30 minutes – and then cooled. This process destroys bacteria and other micro-organisms more completely than pasteurization. Not suitable for cheese-making but good for yogurt-making.

TOP-STIR. Stir the top ½ inch (1 cm) of the milk during cheesemaking in order to keep the cream from rising to the surface immediately after rennet has been added to the milk.

UHT MILK. (Ultra Heat Treated Milk) This milk is first homogenized and then subjected to ultra high tempera-tures – not less than 270°F (132°C) for one minute. This treatment sterilizes the milk but does not affect its taste and colour. Aseptically packed in aluminium foil-lined packs, it keeps for several months if unopened. Known as 'long-life milk'. Not suitable for cheese-making but good for yogurt-making.

WHEY. The green-tinted clear liquid formed when milk coagulates. Whey contains water, milk sugar (lactose), albuminous protein and minerals.

WHOLE MILK. Milk as it comes from the cow, or any other animal, as far as cream content is concerned, i.e., milk from which no cream has been skimmed.

Useful addresses

R. J. Fullwood & Bland Ltd.,
Rennet Works,
Ellesmere,
Salop.
SY12 9DG
Tel: 069 171 2391

This company specialises in cheese rennet and colouring in relatively small quantities, and can provide vegetarian cheese and junket rennet too.

Lotus Food Ltd.,
Unit 3,
Upper Richmond Road,
Putney.
London SW16 2RP
Tel: 01 874 0074

This company can provide vegetarian cheese and junket rennet in relatively small quantities. They also produce a Cheese Making Pack. The pack contains a leaflet with instructions, vegetarian cheese rennet, a sachet of starter and a cheese cloth.

J. J. Blow Limited,
Oldfield Works,
Chatsworth Road,
Chesterfield.
S40 2DJ
Tel: 0246 76635

This company's most attractive product is the 2½ gallon

Dairythene polythene bucket with lid. Stainless steel bowls and buckets are also available.

Divertimenti,
68-70 Marylebone Road Lane,
London W1.

Shop selling a large range of home dairy equipment.

Self-Sufficiency & Smallholding Supplies,
The Old Palace,
Wells,
Somerset.
Tel: 0749 72127

Suppliers of a wide range of dairying and cheesemaking equipment and supplies.

Lincolnshire Smallholders Supplies Ltd.,
Willow Farm,
Thorpe Fendyke,
Wainfleet,
Lincs. PE24 4QH
Tel: 075 486 255

Good range of small scale equipment. List on application.

Anything Goats,
Manor Cottage,
Wretton Road,
Stoke Ferry,
King's Lynn,
Norfolk. PE33 9QJ
Tel: 0366 500065

Goat and dairying supplies.

Chris Hansen Laboratories Ltd.,
476 Basingstoke Road,
Reading. RG2 0QL
Tel: 0734 861056

Cheese and yogurt freeze-dried cultures. Vegetarian cheese rennet. Annatto.

Index

Almond Cheesecake, 102
annatto, 121, 153
Artichoke Bake, 58
Aubergine Cheese Bake, 52
Aubergine Spread/Dip, 35
Avocado, Hot Stuffed, 27
Avocado and Cottage Cheese Pâté, 24
Avocado and Yogurt Cheese Dip, 25

Banana and Cottage Cheese Milk Shake, 92
Blintzes, Russian-Style, 86
buckets, 123
butterfat, 10
buttermilk, commercially cultured, 117, 154
Buttermilk Curd Cheese, 131
Buttermilk Scones with Cream Cheese and Chives, 16

Caerphilly-Style Cheese, 146
calcium, soluble, 118
Cambridge (or York) Cheese, 150
Camembert-Type Cheese, 148
Carob Brownies, Iced, 79
Carob Cheesecake, 106
Carob Cherry Roll, 108
Carrot and Curd Cheese Lettuce Parcels, 70
Carrot Flan, 46
casein, 117, 153
cheese, nutritional value of, 9
Cheese and Spinach Flan, 40
Cheese Balls, 23
cheese boards, 123
cheese cloths, 123
Cheese-Stuffed Tomato Salad, 68
Cheesecake, Continental, 112
Cheesecake, Overnight, 100
Cheesecake Sponge Flan, 114
cheesemaking, acidity in, 119, 153
    variables of, 9
Choux Buns, 30

coagulation, 118
Coconut Dressing, 77
Coeur à la Crème, 84
colander, 123
Colwick Cheese, 142
Cottage Cheese, 127
Cottage Cheese and Cucumber Dressing, 76
Cottage Cheese and Cucumber Mousse, 49
Cottage Cheese and Date Teabread, 96
Cottage Cheese and Sliced Pineapple Salad, 66
Cottage Cheese Bread, 15
Cottage Cheese, Date and Walnut Spread, 33
Cottage Cheese Dip with Crudités, Curried, 28
Cottage Cheese Dressing I, 74
Cottage Cheese Dressing II, 74
Cottage Cheese Omelette, 14
Cottage Cheese Pancakes, 94
Cottage Cheese, Tomato and Orange Salad, 71
Cottage Cheese with Chives and Spring Onions, 29
Coulommiers-Type Cheese, 142
    Herbed, 144
Courgettes Baked with Cheese, 54
Courgettes, Stuffed, 55
cream, 121
Cream Cheese and Yogurt Dip, 36
Cream Cheese Coleslaw, 67
Cream Cheese Dressing, 74
Cream Cheese Icing or Filling, 89
Cream Cheese Pastry Dough, 63
Cream Cheese Scones, 89
Cucumber and Yogurt Cheese Dip, 18
Cucumber Rings, Stuffed, 20
Curd Cheese and Olive Spread, 29
Curd Cheese and Yogurt Dressing, 75
Curd Cheese Dressing, 76

Curd Cheesecake, Baked, 111
Curd Tart, Yorkshire, 110

Date and Cottage Cheese Ice Cream, 93
Dates, Cream Cheese-Stuffed, 19
Double-Cream Cheese, 133

Eggs, Scrambled, with Cottage Cheese, 13
Eggs, Stuffed, 21
equipment, care of, 124

Figs, Fresh, with Cream Cheese and Raspberry Sauce, 83
Fruit Salad, Californian, with Cottage Cheese Dressing, 73

Junket, Devonshire, 80
Simple, 81

lactic acid bacteria, 117
Lactic Curd Cheese, 130
Lactic Goat's Cheese, 141
Leek and Potato Bake, 50
Leek Flan, 47
Lemon Cheese, 138
Lentil Croquettes, 44
Lettuce, Stuffed, 64
Liptauer Cheese, 32

Maids of Honour, 97
milk, 120
    homogenization of, 154
    pasteurization of, 154-55
    raw, 155
    skimmed, 155
    sterilized, 155
    UHT, 155-56
    whole, 156
mixing bowls, 122-23
moulds, 123-24
Mushroom and Vegetable Bake, 60
Mushroom Dip, 36
Mushroom Flan, 45

Nectarine and Raspberry Filled Pancakes, 95

Onion and Cucumber Dip, 37
Orange Gâteau, 107

Pancake Gâteau, St. Clement's, 98
Panir, 138
Pashka, 104
Peach Brûlée, 82
Peach Salad, Stuffed, 69

Pears, Stuffed, 19
Pepper Salad, Stuffed, 72
Plum and Curd Cheese Slice, 91
Potatoes, Baked Stuffed, 39
Potatoes, Boiled, with Cottage or Curd Cheese, 48
Potatoes, Jacket, with Cottage Cheese and Pineapple, 34
Potatoes, Puréed, with Cheese, 59
Potatoes, Scalloped, with Cottage Cheese and Onion, 57
Prunes, Cheese-Stuffed, 19

Raspberry Curd Fool, 85
Ravioli with Ricotta and Spinach Filling, 61
rennet, 118, 120-21
Rennet-Curd Cheese, 128
Ricotta, 134-35
Ricotta-Stuffed Peaches, 90

salt, 121
Scones, Farmhouse Orchard, 88
Single-Cream Cheese, 130
soft cheese, butterfat content of, 10
    flavour variations for, 127
Soup, Creamy Tomato, 22
Sour Cream Dressing, 75
Spaghetti with Ricotta Sauce, 51
Spinach Bake, 56
Spinach Roulade with Tomato Sauce, 42
starter, 117, 155
Strawberry Cheese Mousse, 92
Strawberry Shortcake, 78
Strawberry Sundae, 87

thermometer, 122
Tomato and Cottage Cheese Cocktail, 17
Tomato and Watercress Salad, 65
Tomatoes, Stuffed, 26
Tuma (Ewe's Milk Cheese), 134

utensils, 122

water bath, 124
whey, 118, 119, 156
    collector, 124
Whey Curd Cheese, 134

Yogurt Cheese I, 137
Yogurt Cheese II, 138
Yogurt Cheese Olives, 33
Yogurt Cheese Roll, 139
Yogurt Cheese with Fresh Herbs, 39